Women
OF VIRTUE

Jodi Robinson

CFI
Springville, Utah

This is not an official publication of The Church of Jesus Christ of Latter-day Saints. The opinions and views expressed herein belong solely to the author and do not necessarily represent the opinions or views of Cedar Fort, Inc. Permission for the use of sources, graphics, and photos is also solely the responsibility of the author.

ISBN 13: 978-1-59955-255-2

Published by CFI, an imprint of Cedar Fort, Inc., 2373 W. 700 S., Springville, UT 84663
Distributed by Cedar Fort, Inc., www.cedarfort.com

LIBRARY OF CONGRESS CATALOGING-IN-PUBLICATION DATA

Robinson, Jodi Marie, 1969-
  Women of virtue / Jodi Marie Robinson.
    p. cm.
  ISBN 978-1-59955-255-2
  1. Women--Religious aspects--Church of Jesus Christ of Latter-day Saints.
  2. Christian life--Mormon authors. 3. Body image in women--Religious
aspects--Church of Jesus Christ of Latter-day Saints. I. Title.

  BX8641.R63 2009
  241'.0493--dc22

                          2009002826

Cover design by Jen Boss
Cover design © 2009 by Lyle Mortimer
Edited and typeset by Melissa J. Caldwell

Printed in the United States of America

10 9 8 7 6 5 4 3 2 1

Printed on acid-free paper

True beauty is felt more than it is seen.

Contents

Introduction

"Mom, I look ugly." *What?* I couldn't believe my ears. *What did my beautiful, perfect, wonderful daughter just say?*

"Why would you say that?" I responded with a puzzled glare.

"Well," she said peering down at the floor. "I don't look like the other girls."

"Oh, sweetheart." I sighed, pulling her into me so tightly she could barely breathe. I didn't want to ever let her go. "You don't have to look like anyone. You're beautiful because you are *you*!" I prayed my words were getting through to her as I turned her toward the mirror.

"See," I said. "You have beautiful brown eyes, and silky brown hair, and lips that people pay money to buy. You are just the way God made you. And most of all, you are beautiful . . . in *here*," I said putting my hand to my heart. Seconds passed.

"Thanks, Mom," she said, wrapping her arms around my middle. "I love you. I'm going to go play now." She then brushed the hair off her face, smiled a satisfied smile, and skipped happily out the door.

That speech given to my eight-year-old daughter was the speech of the century because somewhere in some other city, in some other living room, some other mother was giving her daughter the very same speech and as that mother watched her daughter walk away she, too, felt the gripping reality that an experience such as this sadly would not be the last.

If only feeling good about ourselves was as easy as getting a pep talk from a loved one. So, why is feeling good about ourselves sometimes so hard? Because we live in a society that constantly tells us we have to "look" a certain way in order to be happy. But that simply isn't true.

How can we free ourselves from worldly ideals and practices that weigh so heavily on our self-esteem? How can knowing *who* we are help us feel beautiful? And where can we find eternal truths to help teach our daughters (and sons) how to love themselves as God made them to be? In search of answers, I began to study, ponder, and pray; efforts that resulted in the writing of this book.

Although this process has been amazing, it also hasn't been easy. Along the way, I experienced two opposing forces (1) divine inspiration and personal revelation, and (2) utter discouragement and fierce opposition. At times, challenges, conflicts, and temptations made it difficult to move forward. But just as I was ready to give up, minimiracles would happen. Like, when I'd wake up in the middle of the night with thoughts flowing so perfectly into my mind I knew they were not my own. Some days I found answers in the scriptures; verses would suddenly burst with new meaning—meaning I had never before understood. Some answers came through loving priesthood leaders. Others came while attending church or visiting the temple.

Once after an exhaustive search to find an answer to one question in particular, I gave up only to flip open a book weeks later to find the answer staring back at me as if to say, "Oh, Jodi, ye of little faith." Are these just coincidences? Of course not. I know now—without a doubt—when you sincerely seek knowledge and understanding, God holds your hand and leads you to where He wants you to go. When we knock, He answers.

Looking in the mirror, I know I'll never be the kind of beautiful the world wants me to be. And you know what? That's okay. Because I know *real* beauty isn't something that can be airbrushed on. I believe in what our beloved President Hinckley so eloquently stated that "beauty is a thing divine."[1] And "There is none more beautiful, none more inspiring than a [woman] who walks in virtue with an understanding of why she should do so."[2] I believe that whole-heartedly. Nothing this world has to offer—NOTHING—can ever compare to the beauty of virtue.

To see true beauty in ourselves and in others, we can't afford to look out into the world. Instead, we must look to the author and creator of beauty. We must look to God, and *His* definition of beauty is radically different from that of the world's. To God, *virtue* is what makes a woman beautiful. It is what makes her more precious than rubies.

My sincere hope is that this book will inspire you to find the beauty of virtue within yourself—not only for your sake but for the sake of those who follow in your footsteps. For the sake of your daughters, your sons, and young people all over the world who are learning to love themselves and the bodies God gave them; I pray and hope that, as women of faith, we will teach others how precious they truly are by loving who we are and who God made us to be. Let each of us open our eyes to discover within ourselves the beauty of virtue.

NOTES

1. Gordon B. Hinckley, "Rise to the Stature of the Divine within You," *Ensign*, Nov. 1989, 94.

2. Gordon B. Hinckley, "Words of the Prophet: Daughters of the Almighty," *New Era*, Nov. 2003, 4.

Of all the creations of the Almighty
there is none more beautiful,
none more inspiring than a lovely daughter of God
who walks in virtue with an understanding
of why she should do so.

—Gordon B. Hinckley

The Beauty of Virtue

"THERE IS NOTHING IN ALL THIS WORLD AS MAGNIFICENT AS VIRTUE."
—President Gordon B. Hinckley[1]

When my oldest daughter popped into the doorway of my home office, I was hunched over my keyboard humbly defeated by a severe case of writer's block. Standing resolutely at the edge of my desk, looking down at my computer screen, she asked, "So, you're writing about *virtue*. Mom, what exactly *is* virtue?"

"Well," I said, letting out a sigh of desperation, "virtue means being good and making right choices." I figured that answer would suffice the curiosity of a ten-year-old and allow me to get back to staring at my hopelessly empty pages.

"Oh, I get it," my daughter said matter-of-factly. She then spun around and, carefree like a butterfly, hurried back down the hallway to her bedroom. As I watched her golden brown ponytail swish side to side, a flood of emotion swept over me.

"Oh, there is *soooo* much my daughter needs to understand about virtue! Certainly more than any ten-second answer could ever satisfy." Right then, I wanted to call my daughter back, sit her down, and explain how important virtue was; how being true to one's virtue was the only way to truly be happy. I knew the tests my daughter would face in the coming years. I knew staying true to her virtue—staying true to who God made her to be—would be one of her greatest tests. Satan would try to convince her that virtue doesn't matter, when in fact it *does* matter. Virtue

1

matters deeply to the one who matters most—our Savior Jesus Christ. At that very moment, my writer's block ended. My fingers danced across the keyboard, sparked by a brainstorm from my daughter's simple question.

"Mother dear . . . what is virtue?"
"Virtue, dear daughter, is worth more than rubies, more than diamonds or pearls. Virtue upon virtue, virtuous women can change the world."

Can virtuous women *really* make a difference in the world? Do we even understand what virtue is and how it should impact the way in which we live our lives? Understanding virtue is what women of faith must do if they are going to become the women God intends them to be.

VIRTUE MAKES A WOMAN BEAUTIFUL

Marilyn Monroe once said, "In Hollywood a girl's virtue is much less important than her hairdo. You're judged by how you look, not by what you are."[2] I'm afraid that is a sad sentiment but a genuine reflection of the "red carpet" world in which we live. To the world, the beauty of virtue seems to be vanishing. "One would truly need a great and spacious makeup kit to compete with beauty as portrayed in the media all around us."[3] But the truth of the matter is hairdos and makeup kits can never replicate *true* beauty; because true beauty isn't *skin* deep, it's *soul* deep. Beauty is as deep as the whole soul itself. True beauty is found in virtue.

What makes a woman beautiful? It is her soul. Her character. Her substance. Her divine nature. "For [the world] looketh on the outward appearance, but the Lord looketh on the heart" (1 Samuel 16:7). "Virtutem forma decorat" means "beauty adorns virtue."[4] So, what this means is when a woman radiates virtue her beauty is like a "light that gives light to all in the house" (Matthew 5:15). A virtuous woman is a "light pointing toward something far greater than [herself]."[5] This is what makes her beautiful.

DEFINING VIRTUE

To the Lord, "there is nothing in all this world as magnificent as virtue. [Virtue] glows without tarnish. It is precious and beautiful. It is above price. It cannot be bought or sold."[6] These are the words of our beloved President Gordon B. Hinckley five months before he passed away. He explained that although virtue is often equated with chastity and sexual purity it is much broader than that. He defined virtue as the quality of character that brings strength and purity to one's life.[7] In a nutshell, virtue is doing what is right and avoiding what is wrong. It is a quality that creates an inner strength of character that magnifies divine nature and goodness. Beauty is found in those who seek after virtue.

SEEKING VIRTUE

In Philippians 4:8 it says: "If there be any virtue . . . *think on these things*" (emphasis added). But in the thirteenth article of faith we read: "If there is anything virtuous . . . we *seek* after these things" (emphasis added). *Thinking* about virtue and *seeking* after it are two different things. Seeking is an action word. So when we are seeking, we are actively doing something not just passively thinking about something. The thirteenth article of faith teaches that we should be anxiously engaged in *seeking* after virtue and whatsoever things are true, honest, just, pure, lovely, praiseworthy, or of good report. If there is anything virtuous, we should *seek* it out and invite it into our lives. That says a lot about what we should be doing in our day to day goings and comings, doesn't it?

According to our previous definition, to be virtuous we must not only seek out the good but we must avoid the bad, and by doing so we experience an inner strength pushing us along. When we are seeking after virtue we'll feel beautiful! "Really?" you may ask. "How could that be?" Well, you can't help but feel good about yourself when your life is enriched by the strength and purity that comes from virtue. Dressed in virtue, you will always look and feel your best.

WE ARE MORE CONFIDENT BECAUSE OF VIRTUE

Have you ever wondered what meeting the Savior would be like? I have pictured it in my mind hundreds of times. I have imagined myself in a white flowing dress, smiling, as I slowly walk toward Him. I'm nervous, yet exhilarated! I have waited for this moment for as long as I can remember. I am secretly hoping to catch a glimmer in His eye, even a twinkle, just to let me know He recognizes me. As I draw closer to him, I study His face. My eyes look directly into His. He reaches out to me. His gentle hands rest squarely on my shoulders. I look up. The corners of his mouth turn upward into a perfect grin. He then looks at me and I feel his genuine love. He gently pulls me toward him. He embraces me as only a Savior could. I feel the depth of his approval as tears begin to flow down my cheeks. Then, He speaks these words: "Many daughters have done virtuously, but *thou* excellest them all" (Proverbs 31:29, emphasis added). Wouldn't it be wonderful to hear those words—spoken by the Savior himself? We can. And we will, if we will let *virtue* garnish our thoughts unceasingly. Only then will our "*confidence* wax strong in the presence of God" (D&C 121:45, emphasis added). The bottom line is we are more confident when we are living as God wants us to live. We are more confident because of virtue.

Now, change gears for a moment. Think about taking a test; a test that you really didn't study for. Have you ever taken such a test? How did you feel before, during, and after the test? Were you uncomfortable? I had such an experience once in college. I was in the middle of taking a mid-term exam and realized my preparation didn't warrant the kind of confidence needed to get a good grade. In fact, I had prepared so poorly that even reading the test questions was problematic. Hoping to improve my grade the second half of the semester I changed my study habits. During class I took more detailed notes and also bought a syllabus with sample test questions to practice on before the final. By the time the semester ended my confidence was high. I knew I could tackle any test question without fail. And I did.

Well, here we are taking the test of our lifetime. Literally, this is our life test! But are we doing what we should be doing to prepare for the final exam? In other words, are we more concerned about our *worldly* confidence than our *spiritual* confidence?

Are we strengthening our virtue, which will surely give us the kind of confidence required to stand pure and clean before the Lord? Or, in our quest to feel good about ourselves, are we losing a sense of our virtue along the way? We all want to feel good about ourselves. It's important to have a strong self-image. But we have to keep our eyes squarely on our Savior Jesus Christ and on the things that *he* deems important. He is the only way to pass life's test.

Improving our self-image begins with improving our *spiritual* confidence. This requires us to seek after "unceasing" virtue. "Unceasing virtue" will garner the confidence needed to stand before the Lord. And with confidence that is "waxed strong," we will not just *think* we are prepared, for we will *know* we are prepared. Just imagine . . . being prepared to meet God. I don't think one could get any more beautiful than that!

Virtue Is What Makes Us Strong
Think of all the many wonderful qualities associated with being

virtuous: standing as a witness for truth and righteousness; loving others unconditionally; magnifying God-given gifts; reverencing what is holy and sacred; honoring womanhood and motherhood; developing a nurturing nature; having a forgiving heart; being a righteous influence; practicing humility and charity; and abounding in good works. Do any of these virtuous characteristics sound weak to you? Not one. That's because virtue is strong, and virtue makes our character strong. Possessing even a few of these virtuous traits will surely increase that inner strength President Hinckley referred to. Virtue boosts our self-confidence and helps us develop a strong self-image.

BEAUTY IS MORE SPIRITUAL THAN IT IS TEMPORAL

God loves us and wants us to feel positive about who we are and what we have to offer; however, he wants us to recognize the power to feel good about ourselves lies not within some "big and spacious makeup kit," but within our spirits. This power has been with us since the premortal life when we lived as spirit children with God the father. Just like Dorothy in *The Wizard of Oz*, we can access the power of the ruby slippers anytime we need to. We're always wearing them—we just have to remember how to use them.

Wanting to be beautiful and look good is not a bad thing. In fact, we, as women, are programmed to notice beauty and enjoy gathering up beauty wherever we go. Heavenly Father intended women to find joy in beauty. God gave us everything upon this earth for a wise purpose that we might have a fulness of joy. In Doctrine and Covenants 59:15–19, we read: "And inasmuch as ye do these things with thanksgiving, with cheerful hearts and countenances . . . the fulness of the earth is yours . . . the good things which come of the earth . . . both to please the eye and to gladden the heart; Yea, for food and for raiment, for taste and for smell, to strengthen the body and to enliven the soul." The source of beauty comes from the God of our Spirits, Elohim, whose divine nature we embody.[8] This eternal truth teaches us that beauty is far more spiritual than it is temporal.

Women are programmed to appreciate beauty in *all* physical forms. (I have a feeling Heavenly Mother had something to do with this.) Many things of this world please my eyes, gladden my heart, and enliven my soul (not to mention my taste buds). For this reason, I love the handmade, Victorian red quilt that hangs on my banister and the antique white mirrors displayed on my living room wall. I relish in the soft touch of my pink chenille throw and the smooth texture of Hershey's chocolate as it melts in my mouth. Beautiful describes my youngest daughter's amazingly long eyelashes that touch her cheeks as she sleeps as well as my son's naturally curly brown hair. From a quaint, English cottage garden, overflowing with lush plants and flowers to an old, rustic red barn, sitting in a distant pasture, I find treasured beauty in these things. I appreciate a lovely bouquet of wildflowers and the artistic perfection of Japanese orchids. I love the beauty of freshly fallen snow as well as sidewalks covered in fiery red autumn leaves dancing through the wind. In nature, exquisite beauty can be found in the simplicity of morning dew and the complexities of a starry night. *All* of these things are beautiful and they bring me great joy! Beauty is of God. Beauty *is* divine!

DEFINING A VIRTUOUS WOMAN

It would be impossible to perfectly define a beautiful and virtuous woman and describe exactly what she looks like. But for the purpose of this book, I will try to picture how I see her in my mind. A beautiful and virtuous woman is a rare gem in today's world. She exemplifies all that is good, gracious, lovely, and kind. Her influence is limitless, endless, and timeless. She is the champion of heavenly causes. She forsakes the popular for the praiseworthy. She focuses on being true rather than being trendy. She strives for exactness as she applies gospel principles. She is intelligent and possesses an inner strength because she knows who she is. She strives for purity and confidently relies on the atoning power of her Savior. She desires to live and lead by the virtue of her divinely given talents and virtuous traits. Serving other, by sharing her talents gives her great joy. She senses her innate ability to influence others in righteousness, and the strength of her spirit is felt by everyone with whom she associates. She is humble in her abilities and gives credit to the Lord for all her accomplishments. She loves the Lord with all her might, mind, and strength. She faithfully obeys the prophet and willingly follows the counsel of her Church leaders. Her values are the Lord's values. She understands that Heavenly Father values a virtuous woman and considers her worth to be priceless.

A virtuous woman is not discouraged by her imperfections. She knows the Lord has power to make weak things become strong. She uses the atonement in her daily life. She seeks to forgive and to be forgiven.

She is not a "worldly" woman—not in her desires, not in her deeds, not in her dress. As she faces her Goliaths and personal tests of virtue, she senses a higher purpose deep within her soul, revealing that she has come into the world "for such a time as this" (Esther 4:14). She abounds in good works as she influences others by her virtuous example. Friends, family, and even strangers are blessed to be in her presence *not* because of who she is or what she looks like but because of how she makes others feel when they are with her.

Helen Keller said, "The most beautiful things in the world cannot be seen or even touched, they must be felt with the heart."[9] This is what being beautiful is about. To a virtuous woman of God, beauty is something that is felt far more than it is seen.

True Beauty Is Felt More than Seen

Recently, my paternal grandmother passed away. She was full of life and energy until she had a stroke that left her legs paralyzed. Three days before she died, I went to visit her. Slowly opening the door to her bedroom, I announced, "I'm here, Grandma. I came for a visit." Hearing my voice, her eyebrows lifted as she tilted her head towards the door. A ray of sunlight beamed through the curtain, catching the edges of her salt and pepper hair and creating a halo effect. I immediately crawled into bed next to her and nestled my body right up against hers. She felt warm and soft as a grandma should.

On my way into her bedroom, I had picked up a special photo album that was sitting on her kitchen table. My uncle had compiled it, and I was anxious to show it to her.

"Grandma, you're going to love these pictures," I said turning to the first page. The album contained family photos from Grandma's eighty-five years of life. One of my favorites was Grandma's and Grandpa's engagement photo. The year was 1943.

"Oh, look how handsome Grandpa was in his Navy uniform. And look how beautiful you look, Grandma!" I said, touching her gently on the arm. She smiled and rested her head against my shoulder. "And Grandma," I said quietly, "you are *still* beautiful." Not able to speak she looked into my eyes. She smiled as she placed her hand on mine. I then began to study the intricacies of her hands. They were wrinkled and worn with age spots and, yet, they were the most beautiful hands I had ever seen. Why? Because of what those hands did for me and how they made me feel. They rocked me when I was a baby. Cuddled me, hugged me, and consoled me. Those hands taught me how to crochet, sew, and make wheat bread. Those hands were heavenly hands, always busy doing something for someone.

Right then, Grandma motioned to me and pointed to her knees. "Oh, do you need me to adjust your nightgown, Grandma?" I asked. "Yes," she said softly. So I set the photo album down and walked to the edge of the bed. I tugged at her white cotton nighty, carefully repositioning her legs, legs that could no longer walk. As I gently rubbed her legs, I began to think about all the things those legs had done in eighty-five years. In my mind I imagined her standing in the kitchen baking. That was quite an undertaking considering her house was always full of people waiting to eat—family members, neighborhood kids, and even strangers Grandpa brought home from the university where he taught. I imagined Grandmother as a young mom, happily chasing after eleven children, and later as a grandmother chasing after fifty-four grandchildren and then thirty-six great-grandchildren. And then I pictured her, of all things, riding a tandem bicycle (a bicycle built for two); a bike Grandpa had purchased when they were in their fifties. Oh, how they loved riding that bike! Then I thought about the pictures we saw in the photo album; so many of which were of Grandma holding a child in her lap. Yes, Grandma had strong legs. And they were beautiful legs even though they had never strolled down a catwalk or a runway.

Looking into her steel-blue eyes, I asked, "Are you tired, Grandma?" She nodded yes. Even under physical strain, I noticed how her eyes sparkled with a life well-lived. I decided my grandmother's beauty was definitely in her eyes. Gently, I covered her with a soft blanket and watched her drift off to sleep. As she lay there peacefully, the words to one of my favorite songs came to mind: "And no woman from a movie or TV could ever hope to be as beautiful as she."[10] Grandma taught me a lot about what it means to be beautiful because her beauty was felt far more than it was seen. Thank you, Grandma, for letting me see in you the beauty of virtue.

NOTES

1. Gordon B. Hinckley, "Words of the Prophet: Daughters of the Almighty," *New Era*, Nov. 2003, 4.

2. Marilyn Monroe, "Quotes on Virtue," http://www.notable-quotes.com/v/

virtue_quotes.html.

3. Jeffrey R. Holland, "To Young Women," *Liahona*, Nov. 2005, 28.

4. Robert Hughes, "When Beauty Was Virtue," http://www.time.com/time/magazine/article/0,9171,1001514-2,00.html.

5. Tom Gilson, "The Beauty of Virtue," http://www.thinkingchristian.net/C278308471/E20070307072112/index.html

6. Gordon B. Hinckley, "How Can I Become the Woman of Whom I Dream?" *Ensign*, May 2001, 93.

7. Gordon B. Hinckley, "True to the Faith," *BYU Speeches*, 18 September, 2007.

8. Henry B. Eyring, "Walk in the Light," *Ensign*, May 2008, 123.

9. Helen Keller, "Classic Quotes," http://www.quotationspage.com/quote/30187.html.

10. Cherie Call, *Beneath These Stars*, "She," 2005.

2

More Precious than Rubies

WHO CAN FIND A VIRTUOUS WOMAN?
FOR HER PRICE IS FAR ABOVE RUBIES.
—Proverbs 31:10

To the Lord, the worth of a virtuous woman is "far above rubies" (Proverbs 31:10). But do we *really* understand how precious rubies really are? As the saying goes, "Diamonds are a girl's best friend." But did you know that a three carat ruby is actually more rare than a three carat diamond?

There are three types of precious gems: diamonds, sapphires, and rubies. Rubies (which are usually red) are made of the same mineral as sapphires (which are blue). Rubies and sapphires are both made of the mineral corundum. Only slight variations of certain elements (such as chrome, iron, titanium, or vanadium) determine whether a stone will be ruby red or sapphire blue. A ruby is not a ruby by chance. It was destined to become one.

So, what makes a ruby more precious than diamonds or sapphires? Well, to form a ruby with brilliant, red color and few or zero impurities, perfect environmental conditions must be met. For example, chrome is the element which gives the ruby its wonderful, vibrant, red color; however, chrome is also the element that causes fissures, or cracks, inside the crystals. So, too much chrome, or not enough, can cause imperfections. Any imperfection affects the size of the ruby as well as its color. Ultimately, a ruby of substantial size, with few flaws, is a rare occurrence in nature and brings a hefty price at auction—sometimes, even more than diamonds.[1]

So, is it any wonder the Lord equates a woman's worth, not with diamonds—a gem that holds great significance by worldly standards; and not with sapphires for, although they are precious, they are not the rarest of the gems. Yet, even still compared to one of the rarest finds of all—rubies—*a virtuous woman is priced far above them.*

REMEMBER WHO YOU ARE

Why is it important to remember how precious rubies are? How precious *we* are? One good reason: self-doubt. And we've all experienced it. Just because we aren't pimply teenagers anymore doesn't mean we aren't *ever* going to feel insecure. (Don't we wish!) Take the simple act of thumbing through a magazine. The minute we see a model the size of a french fry we wonder, "Is that what I'm supposed to look like?" (Give me a break! We're supposed to eat french fries, not look like them.) It's important to remember we didn't have negative feelings about ourselves when were in the premortal life because we lived in God's presence. Living with God was a perfect environment and that environment didn't allow us to experience fissures and cracks. But living here in mortality we are subjected to the influences of the adversary, and because of that exposure, we do experience fissures and cracks in our everyday lives.

Don't you wish sometimes you could just remember exactly what living with God felt like? Wouldn't it be great if we could set up a chat room with God so whenever we felt a little "cracked" we could dial in and say, "Can you tell me one more time how precious rubies really are?" Well, the good news is we can! We can create our own personal chat room with Heavenly Father by learning eternal truths about who we are and who he created us to be, and then *remembering* these eternal truths on a daily basis. These truths will teach us the doctrine of our eternal self-worth. They will give us something to hang on to as we journey through mortality. Yes, we've passed through the veil. Yes, we are separated from God and from his son, Jesus Christ. But through the scriptures and living prophets and apostles, God reconnects us with deity. He reminds us that we *are* children of God. We are Heavenly Father's offspring (Genesis 1:27). God the Father loves us so very much. Each person on this earth is so valuable to Him that even the very hairs on our heads are numbered (Matthew 10:29–31). Our Father knows everything about us. He is familiar with all our ways (Psalms 139:3). He knows when we sit down and when we rise up and he knows our thoughts even before we think them (Psalm 139:2).

Our Father knew us before we were even conceived (Jeremiah 1:4–5). Our spirits *are* eternally connected to deity. These eternal truths should always remind us of who we are and who we've always been. Understanding these truths and remembering them will make us happy. Actually, they should make us gloriously happy!

THE "IDEAL" WOMAN OBSESSION

Sadly, remembering who we are isn't as simple as it should be, because the world in which we live diminishes the *value* of a woman's virtue. Celebrity culture and powerful media images make virtue look like an antique, like something from a bygone era. Our society is obsessed with an unrealistic "ideal" of what a woman should look like, act like, and dress like. This "ideal" is far from virtuous. It downplays the importance of a woman's *spiritual* makeup and plays up the importance of her *physical* makeup.

Thirty years ago the "ideal" woman was the "bring-home-the-bacon-never-let-you-forget-you're-a-man" sort of woman. Well, now that woman's on steroids! Today, society has dished up an even better "ideal woman" who not only cooks up the bacon, but owns her own bacon manufacturing plant. She lives in decorator showroom and looks and dresses like a centerfold model even though she gave birth to eight children, who, by the way, are all Harvard bound even though they haven't graduated yet from grade school. Hmmm. Is this the "ideal" we're supposed to buy into? Because it isn't only *not* real, but it's confusing. (Not to mention exhausting.)

So is there hope for our confused and troubled world? Of course there is. There is hope if we are willing to start back at the beginning; if we are willing to focus on who we were in the beginning, who our Father is, and who He wants us to become, and not focus so much on who the world wants us to become. President Gordon B. Hinckley offered this counsel: "There is a great reason to have hope, for there is a remedy. . . . We would do well to emphasize the kinds of virtues celebrated by the apostle Paul: 'Whatsoever things are *true . . . honest . . . just . . . pure . . . lovely*, [and] *of good report*; if there be any *virtue*, and if there be any praise, think on *these* things' (Philippians 4:8-9, emphasis added)."[2] Yes, there is a remedy for our hopeless confusion. But this remedy can't be bought, sold, or borrowed. It can't be found in a beauty procedure or a lotion. In fact, it has nothing to do with the world. This remedy, my dear sister and friend, is virtue. It is in the purity of virtue we will find our "perfect brightness of hope" (2 Nephi 31:20). Hope for a strong self-image. Hope for better future. Hope for happiness, joy, and peace.

Virtue is that special something far more precious and more real than any "ideal obsession" this world has to offer. President Hinckley said it best: "There is no substitute under the heavens for personal virtue."[3] Virtuous beauty is priceless.

PROTECTING OUR ETERNAL IDENTITY

Something priceless cannot be easily replaced, so it must be protected, guarded, and sheltered. Our virtue is priceless. For this reason we must protect our virtue from the influences of the world. How can we protect it? Because we have passed through the veil, we have forgotten everything about the virtue of who we were before we came here. At the moment we were born, the premortal life became a faded memory. There was and is a great purpose in this "forgetting," for we needed to come to earth to be tested and to develop faith. This forgetting, however, sometimes makes it hard to remember what we came here to do. Especially as we go about our daily lives and as we encounter struggles and trials that wear and tear on our self-esteem.

As I mentioned earlier, living in mortality subjects us to the fissures and cracks sustained by worldly influences. Satan knows this. He works hard to do whatever he can to confuse us about who we are, because he knows we can't remember our life before, when we walked and talked with God. He doesn't want us to remember what we are destined to become. And Satan uses this "forgetting" to his advantage. What we need to do to protect our eternal identity from the influences of the adversary is to simply *remember*—remember who we are and the virtue of who we have always been.

BELOVED DAUGHTERS OF GOD

And just who are we? "We are *beloved* spirit daughters of God, and our lives have meaning, purpose, and direction."[4] Beloved means to be singled out as the object of God's affection. Isn't that beautiful! We can't waste a minute of this earth life to remember this because too much is at stake. We have to remember it now! As daughters of God we are the "object of God's heavenly affection" and upon *this* eternal truth alone we must base our self-worth. Our eternal destiny depends on it; for if we forget who we are, we may miss out on blessings and opportunities to develop our spiritual character; the character in which our eternal identity is found.

It would be impossible to measure Heavenly Father's love for us. I know I have felt a deep and abiding love from my *own* father. I can't see it, but I know it is deep and it is real. So, how does our Heavenly Father's perfect affection compare? Heavenly Father's love for us is a divine affection that can't match anything this world has to offer. God's love for us is unparalleled because he knows everything about us (Psalm 139:3). He knows our strengths; our weaknesses; what makes us happy; what makes us sad; he knows our imperfections and he loves us anyway! Heavenly Father's beloved affection is immeasurable, and his love is perfect. If we can rely on this truth alone when we are feeling down and less than perfect, we will feel the reality of who we are and begin to see the possibilities of our eternal potential. In God's eyes, we are valued, loved, and cherished, not because of what our physical bodies look like but because of what our spirits look like. And our spirits were made in the image of God. We are His beloved spirit daughters.

Now contrast Heavenly Father's divine affection to Satan's deception that a woman's worth comes from being the object of man's affection. You see, to the adversary it is a woman's physical body that makes her beloved. The adversary does not want us to know we are beloved simply because we are spirit daughters of God, made in His image. He'd like us to forget that altogether, and he works hard to get us to do so. In fact, Satan is responsible for those fissures and cracks in our self-perception that make us believe we're "too" this or "too" that; or that we don't have enough "this" or we have too much of "that." He wants us focused on our bodies as objects—a falsehood that leads to feelings of low self-esteem, degradation, disappointment, and disillusionment.

The only way to really feel good about how we look and who we are is to know deep within the core of our being (to feel it deep inside) that we are beloved by God because we are made in his image. If we are going to know this for sure, we have to look to heavenward. We have to look to God and not out into the world to value our self-worth.

One of the places we can feel beloved is in the temple. The temple is a holy place where God's pure love shines through. Here is an experience from a friend of mine named Sharon, who told me how she went to the temple seeking to feel God's love for her.

Years ago, I was struggling with my self-image. For some time, I had secretly wrestled with feelings of self-doubt. I had a wonderful husband and children. I had much to be grateful for. But inside I was struggling. I decided to fast and attend the temple and seek help from my Heavenly Father. I waited all through the temple session hoping to feel something. Although being in the temple helped me feel more peaceful, the answer I was expecting had not yet come. I was a little disappointed. Then, as I was getting ready to leave the dressing room I passed by a mirror. I looked at myself in that mirror and I'll never forget the words that came into my mind. "Sharon, you are beautiful because you are made in the image of God. His image is in your countenance. You look like your Father." It was as soft as a whisper. That was my answer and I knew the Lord had heard my prayer.

Being created in the image of an Almighty God—can you get more beautiful than that!

Quiet whisperings of the Spirit can come to each of us as we seek confirmation from the Lord about who we are. Let us go often to the temple. Let us go to the Lord's House to remember who we are and who we have the potential to become.

Know Who You Are
Consider these words from Elder Jeffrey R. Holland:

I want you to feel the reality of what that means, to know who you truly are. You are literally a spirit daughter of heavenly parents with a divine nature and an eternal destiny. That surpassing truth should be fixed deep in your soul and be fundamental to every decision you make. . . . There could never be a greater authentication of your dignity, your worth, your privileges, and your promise. . . . Because of this divine heritage you, along with all of your spiritual sisters and brothers, have full equality in His sight and are empowered through obedience to become a rightful heir in His eternal kingdom.[5]

These words from President Holland remind us that our worth is immeasurable, not because of what we look like; not because our bodies are a certain shape or size; not because of the clothes we wear, the house we live in, or the talents we have. All on our own, with nothing but the skin we're in, without a hint of doubt, *we are beloved.*

Building Your Self-worth on a Sure Foundation
When seeking to improve our self-worth, we must first remember to

build on a sure foundation. There is a famous song, well-known among children, about a foolish man who builds his house upon the sand, and when the rains come down, the house on the sand washes away. The wise man chooses to build his house on the rocks. When the rains come down, his house stands firm. From this simple song we learn the importance of building our self-worth, not on worldly sand, but on "sure" foundations (Helaman 5:12). Sure foundations keep women true to their identity as daughters of God. Wise women know this. Wise women will always look to Christ as the "anchor" of their souls, and they will build their self-esteem from there.

CHAMPIONED BY CHRIST

Next, we must remember Christ is our champion. During a very difficult trial in my life, I was on my knees several times a day asking Heavenly Father to bless me with peace. But peace did not come. I decided to ask my husband for a priesthood blessing. In faith, I knew I would receive an answer. My answer came, in fact, in the first few words of the blessing: "Jodi, the Lord knows who you are." I could feel tingles and I knew. I knew the Lord heard and understood my pleadings. I knew, somehow, some way, Christ would champion my cause. James E. Talmage said, "The world's greatest champion of woman and womanhood is Jesus the Christ."[6] How does knowing that Christ is our champion make you feel? It makes me want to jump for joy!

The Lord will champion anyone who desires to come unto Him. He is a true hero, a knight whose armor shines brighter than the noonday sun. He is a champion to all of us because He overcame the world for us. "By the virtue of the blood which [He] spilt," He promises to plead our case before the Father, as any true champion would do (D&C 38:4). When we are feeling low, when we are feeling down, when we feel that the world is weighing down heavily upon us, we can get on our knees and ask for help from above. "Lord, help me feel good about myself. Help me love myself. Help me see myself the way you see me; help me love my body and be grateful for the gift you have given me. Help me feel whole." And He will help you. He really will.

CHRIST WILL VOUCH FOR US

Third, we must remember that through the miracle of the Atonement our Savior, Jesus Christ, will vouch for us. I learned what this meant a few years ago while getting ready for Ward temple Night, and I couldn't find my temple recommend.

"Where could it be?" I said disappointingly to my husband. "I had it last month, but where did I put it?" My husband suggested I call the bishop.

"Oh, I would be so embarrassed," I said. "I'm the Relief Society President, for heaven's sake. That's just great. Here I am on Ward temple Night and I'm caught without oil in my lamp!" As the minutes ticked by, I finally got up the nerve to call. My bishop was so kind. He said, "Meet me at the temple a few minutes early and I'll vouch for you." Not knowing exactly what my bishop meant, I trusted him and followed his instructions.

Once inside the lobby of the temple, I sought out my bishop. Together we found the temple president. Bishop Larsen introduced me jokingly as the Relief Society president who had no oil in her lamp. "President, do you think we can let her in?" The temple president looked at me quite seriously and said, "Come with me." We followed him down the hallway and my heart was beating so fast I could hardly swallow. (I seriously was wondering if they were leading me to some special place where the "unprepared" virgins were kept.) We, of course, ended up in just an ordinary office where the bishop verified some paperwork and after a few minutes my bishop turned to shake my hand and said, "You're good to go, Jodi. I vouched for you." I was so happy to hear those words. I was grateful to be in the temple that day. Gratitude filled my heart because of a kind and loving bishop who "vouched" for me.

All through the endowment session, those words played over and over in my mind. "I'll vouch for you. I'll vouch for you." I had never before thought about the Savior's Atonement in that way. But that is exactly what the Savior will do for me if I live up to my covenants. I could almost hear Christ saying, "Father, this is Jodi Robinson. I'll vouch for her. Let her in."

Our Savior died for us He took upon him our sins. He bore our griefs and sorrows, and did so willingly. After all we can do, our Savior will vouch for us. All he asks of us is that we come unto him by coming out of the world. "And verily I say unto thee that thou shalt lay aside the things of this world, and seek for the things of a better" (D&C 25:10).

Sisters, Satan *won't* vouch for us. He will abandon us before the competition even starts to get heated. He will leave us unsupported, all alone without any back up. If you ever doubt this just look at someone's life who is wrapped up in sin and you'll know this to be true. Satan takes something sacred, contorts it, twists it, turns it, and crumples it up, and throws it on the floor. Then he walks away and never looks back. Satan can't repair virtue, and he certainly can't restore it. Satan can't champion who we are or who we can become because he doesn't have the power to do so. But Christ can, and he will champion our cause! He won't only champion us, but he will vouch for us and *never* will he forsake us. "Upheld by His righteous omnipotent hand" Christ is our champion.[7]

BE CLOSE ENOUGH TO TOUCH THE SAVIOR

The fourth thing we must remember is to live close to the Savior— close enough that we could reach out and touch Him. And so I ask, "How is your relationship with the Savior? Are you close enough in your spiritual associations with Him that *you* could reach out and touch Him?"

Imagine for a moment the woman in the scriptures, who was stricken with a blood disease for twelve years (Luke 8:43). This woman desperately wanted to be cured. Undoubtedly, she experienced great sorrow and had given up hope so many times before. She was an outcast, considered to be unclean even among her own people (Mark 5:25–34). She must have been so lonely. With overwhelming faith and compelling courage, she sought healing from the miracle worker named Jesus. She believed this man could physically heal her. At the risk of exposing others to her disease, she was not supposed to be among crowds, but after hearing about Jesus' miracles she found the courage to venture out into the streets where Jesus walked. With faith as her focus, she reached out and lightly touched the hem of His garment (Luke 8:44–47).

Now, focus on the scene. It is a crowded street. People are moving about in close quarters. Christ is walking along with his Apostles when he turns to them and asks, "Who touched me?" Dumbfounded, they responded saying, "Master, what do you mean 'who touched you'? Of course, people are touching you, we are in the middle of a crowded street." But Christ knew exactly what He was asking. He knew "someone" had touched him with a specific purpose in mind (Matthew 9:21). He could feel it. Someone had touched him for the purpose of being healed; for at the moment Christ was touched, he felt virtue leave him (Luke 8:46). He knew the difference between someone casually brushing against Him and someone seeking to be made whole. He knew the woman who had touched Him had the faith that He could heal her. And Christ did heal her . . . by the *virtue* of who He was.

You and I can be made whole physically, spiritually, emotionally, and mentally by the virtue of who Christ is. We can literally feel the Savior's virtue flowing through our veins, *if* we draw close enough to touch Him. In seeking to define ourselves, to be beautiful, to feel worthy, to feel accepted, to be loved, we must set our eyes squarely on Christ; for if we "take our eye off of [the Savior] and let the world define us, it is as if we are 'walking in darkness at noon-day (see D&C 95:6)'."[8] Let us walk close enough to touch Him.

God's Identity Guarantee

Each of us at some time or another asks the question: Who am I? But the question we need to be asking is: *Whose* am I? Can you feel the difference? The first question seems open-ended, as if there is no beginning and no end. But, the second question immediately connects us with eternity. Asking "whose are we" or "to whom do we belong" draws our focus to an eternal realm where we are acquainted with deity.

When we remember to do these things: (1) build our self-image on the sure foundation of Jesus Christ; (2) desire to have Christ champion our cause; (3) understand that Christ will always vouch for us; and (4) draw close enough to touch Him, we will then receive the Lord's Identity Guarantee. And guess what? It comes with a warranty! So whenever we feel "cracked" or "broken," Christ's love can mend us and make us whole.

Being Authentic

Much has been said in the last two decades about living an "authentic" life. But in order for us to be truly authentic we must be *true* to our true identity. Let's take this one step further—we must be *true* to our virtue. For the Lord teaches us "that which [is] most dear and precious above all things . . . is . . . virtue" (Moroni 9:9). By being true to our virtue, we are being true to our God and what He deems most precious. And what is more authentic than living your truth as a virtuous daughter of God? After all, only a virtuous you is truly an authentic *you*! Now that is authenticity!

Elder M. Russell Ballard of the Quorum of the Twelve Apostles said: "Of this you may be certain: the Lord especially loves righteous women—women who are not only faithful but filled with faith, women who are optimistic and cheerful because they know who they are and where they are going, women who are striving to live and serve as women of God."[9] Yes, there will be those who will choose to follow the ways of the world. "I'm just being me and expressing my individuality," someone will say to defend her style of dress. "It's just who I am," another might proclaim to defend a lifestyle choice. "Changing my looks isn't going to change me," a voice may rationalize. These are voices of women trying to find themselves. But they are looking in the wrong places. They are looking into the world to define who they are. And, sadly, they will be deceived. Too many are trying to find themselves by changing what they look like on the outside while forgetting that *who* they are can only be found on the *inside*. Those who look to authenticate who they are by chasing after worldly identities will never feel a sense of eternal authenticity.

Being Out of Step with the World

If we desire to be authentic, we must live "out of step" with the world. How do we live out of step with the world? We begin by accepting the doctrine that we are literal children of God and then act the way literal children of God are supposed to act. If we fail to do this "the messages of the world will confuse us and confound us . . . . [Only] true doctrine, understood and *held onto*, will give us the strength to let go of the falsehoods of the world."[10] Many falsehoods promise happiness yet garner mediocre results. *True* happiness only comes when we hold onto true doctrine and let go of worldly falsehoods. Wendy Watson Nelson, wife of the Apostle Russell M. Nelson, said during Women's Conference 2007, "If we are following the Lord, we will feel increasingly out of step with the world. In fact, perhaps an early clue that there is something not quite right in our lives is if we are feeling a little too comfortable with the world, if we are looking and acting a little too much like the women of the world."[11] (I'll be the first to admit that I *do* feel a little "out of step" with the world—more and more each and every day. Thanks to Sister Nelson's talk I am reassured that this is a good thing!)

A Test Is Coming

President Heber C. Kimball prophesied to the saints before the turn of the twentieth century. President Hinckley quoted him as saying: "The time is coming when we will be mixed up in these now peaceful valleys to that extent that it will be difficult to tell the face of a Saint from the face of an enemy to the people of God. Then . . . look out for the great sieve, for there will be a great sifting time, and many will fall; for I say unto you there is a test, a *test*, a TEST coming, and who will be able to stand?" President Hinckley added to this thought: "I am inclined to think the time is here and that the test lies in our capacity to live the gospel rather than adopt the ways of the world." Yes, we live in difficult times, but "we have a responsibility and a challenge to take our places in the world . . . [and] this does not require a surrender of standards."[12] Because of the gift of agency and the plan of happiness, the choice is ours. We can choose whether we surrender to worldly standards or hold strong and faithful to the Lord's iron rod.

> It is easy enough to be virtuous
> When nothing tempts you to stray,
> When without or within no voice of sin
> Is luring your soul away;
> But it's only a negative virtue
> Until it is tried by fire,
> And the life that is worth the honors of earth
> Is the one that resists desire.[13]

Our virtue is strengthened each time we resist temptation. It is in the face of temptation when resisting is needed the most. When the adversary comes a knocking, let us dare to stand firm in our convictions. Let us not surrender who we are!

Surrendering is not the word that comes to mind when I think of Sheri Dew, former first counselor in the Relief Society General Presidency. Years ago, I heard her give a youth fireside. She related the following story: Sister Dew said a friend of hers once said to her, "Sheri, Satan must say every morning as your feet hit your bedroom floor, 'Oh great! She's awake again!'" Isn't that fantastic! Can't you just envision Satan yelling, "I hate when that happens!" That is exactly how we need to make Satan feel about us. He needs to know we are virtuous, intelligent, capable, and strong forces for good. He needs to know his temptations *cannot* and *will not* prevent us from walking in paths of virtue, and every time he comes for us we must show an even stronger resistance. We must do this at all times, and in all things, and in all places and be true to who God made us to be.

VIRTUE INTEGRITY

Think of this principle of "being true" to who you are as having virtue integrity. Virtue integrity means your thoughts, feelings, and actions are in harmony with your heart. Appearance, physical health, language, media choices, music choices, philosophies on dating, marriage, vocational pursuits, personal interests, and body image are *all* consistent with the Lord's values. To a young woman or woman with virtue integrity, even something as simple as buying a swimsuit becomes an opportunity to show who she is and to whom she belongs. Without question her choices are in line with the standards in *For the Strength of Youth* (even if she's not a youth). She honors the principles and standards of the gospel. She honors the priesthood and strives to follow the counsel of the apostles and prophets with exactness. A woman with virtue integrity sets a virtuous example for her daughters and granddaughters, as she lives, leads, and teaches the principles of virtue by word and deed.

Elder Joseph B. Wirthlin said when you have integrity you are "incapable of being false." You're "incorruptible."[14] Think about what that means. When we have integrity, we are incapable of putting forth a false image. And let's face it. The world is all about false images. When we have virtue integrity we don't seek to be something the Lord desires us not to be.

Elder Jeffrey R. Holland pleads: "Be a woman of Christ. Cherish your esteemed place in the sight of God. He needs you. This Church needs you. The world needs you."[15] President Gordon B. Hinckley continually encouraged us to be the best we can be:

> You have such tremendous potential. . . . Every one of you was endowed by your Father in Heaven with a tremendous capacity to do good in the world. Train your minds and your hands that you may be equipped to serve well in the society of which you are a part. Cultivate the art of being kind, of being thoughtful, of being helpful. Refine within you the quality of mercy which comes as a part of the divine attributes you have inherited. . . . In summary, try a little harder to measure up to the divine within each of you.[16]

May we remember *always* how precious rubies are! It's the only way we'll ever truly be happy.

Notes

1. International Colored Gemstone Association, "Ruby," http://www.gemstone.org/gem-by-gem/english/ruby.html.

2. Gordon B. Hinckley, *Standing for Something* (New York City: Random House, 2000), xxi-xxii.

3. Gordon B. Hinckley, "The Body is Sacred," *New Era*, Nov. 2006, 2.

4. Relief Society Declaration, emphasis added.

5. Holland, "To Young Women."

6. James E. Talmage, as quoted in M. Russell Ballard, "Be Strong in the Lord," *Ensign*, Jul. 2004, 8.

7. "How Firm a Foundation," *Hymns,* No. 85.

8. Barbara Day Lockhart, "Divine Doctrines, Divine Reality," in *Rise Up To the Divinity Within You* (Salt Lake City: Deseret Book, 2007), 49.

9. M. Russell Ballard, "Here am I, Send Me," 2001 BYU Women's Conference (http://ce.byu.edu/cw/womensconference/archive/2001/ballard_mrussell.html).

10. Carolyn Rasmus, *Simplify: A Guide to Caring for the Soul* (Salt Lake City: Deseret Book, 2007), 102.

11. Wendy Watson Nelson, "For Such a Time as This," *Talks from the 2007 Women's Conference* (Salt Lake City: Deseret Book), 2008, 7–8.

12. Gordon B. Hinckley, "A City Upon A Hill." *Ensign*, Jul. 1990, 2.

13. Ella Wheeler Wilcox, 1850–1919 [need more info.]

14. Joseph B. Wirthlin, "Personal Integrity," *Ensign*, May 1990, 30.

15. Holland, "To Young Women."

16. Gordon B. Hinckley, "The Light within You," *Ensign*, May 1995, 99.

3

Walking in Paths of Virtue

Did you know Doctrine and Covenants 25 holds a remarkable secret? It answers the life-changing question: "What does God expect of me?" I discovered this one night as I was hiding in my home office.

"MO-OM! Where are you?" I heard my children say. They were looking for me, and I dared barely breathe. I carefully slid my foot against the door blocking it just in case they tried to enter. Right then I heard, "DA-ad, where's mom?"

Oh, he wouldn't dare rat me out, I thought. *Not after a day like I had had.*

"Leave Mom alone!" I heard him say. *"Ahhhh. Thank goodness."* I breathed a sigh of relief as the sound of tiny footsteps disappeared up the stairs. *Alone at last!* All cozied up in my bright, cotton-candy pink, fleece bathrobe (the one my children are embarrassed for me to be seen in), I sank effortlessly into my black swivel chair. I then reached into my pocket, pulled out the last nibble of my king-size Hershey bar and happily devoured the velvety morsel as it melted in my mouth. It was like a river of relief. After a full day of changing dirty diapers, corralling rambunctious children, and cleaning up cat hair, my spirit needed a boost. So I began surfing the Web for something uplifting to read. That's when I discovered a talk given by President Gordon B. Hinckley. In it, I read this poignant question: *"What does God expect of me [and every other woman]?"*[1] My eyes settled on those words like a plane landing on a runway. I sat forward in my chair anxious to know the answer.

But wait a minute, I thought. *I already knew the answer. Didn't I?* Being a bit curious, I scooted closer to my monitor and intently read out loud: "Some of the things that God expects of [you] and of every other woman—in fact, of each of us—are set forth in this beautiful revelation." President Hinckley was referring to Doctrine and Covenants 25. Now, I knew section 25 was commonly known as the "elect lady" section where the Lord called Emma Smith, wife of the prophet Joseph Smith, an "elect lady" and promised her blessings if she kept the commandments. But I had never considered it to be an exact outline showing what God expected of women. I was intrigued. If I wanted to understand what President Hinckley was saying, and what the Lord was saying, I needed to study section 25. So I got out my scriptures.

Verse one: "Hearken, unto the voice of the Lord your God, while I speak unto you, [Jodi Robinson,] my daughter. " I read and thought to myself, *I'm prepared to hearken.*

Verse two: "A revelation I give unto you concerning my will; and if thou art faithful . . ." *Well, I'm being faithful.* "And **walk in the paths of virtue** before me. . ." *STOP!* Had there been a band in the room as I read that phrase, I would have heard a big *ta-dah*! Walk in the paths of virtue! These words were like a symphony to me! Why hadn't I noticed them before? (I swear I had a hot flash, but it was probably just the fleece.) Obviously the next question was: "How does a woman walk in the paths of virtue?" Well, guess what? I read all sixteen verses and, in each verse, I found treasured gems of wisdom. Section 25 was a call from the Lord to "walk in the paths of virtue" and each verse was a stepping stone outlining how to accomplish this. From being a better wife, daughter, sister, and friend and a more devoted servant of the Lord, section 25 held valuable insight about what God expects of women. From that point on I was hooked, and my journey to walk in paths of virtue had begun.

A RARE TREASURE

Something wonderful happens to my psyche when I think of Doctrine and Covenants 25 being given to a woman. Section 25 is the only known recorded scriptural revelation given directly to a woman and that makes it a rare treasure (and I know women appreciate rare treasures).[2] Now, that's not to say that essential gospel truths are less effective when they are taught by men. Why, that would be silly! Where would we be without the valuable teachings of Nephi, Jacob, King Benjamin, Moroni, Moses, and Abraham? Their teachings apply to male, female, old, and young. But let's be honest. Few stories in the scriptures are about women, let alone specifically written *for* women; so, to me, this section of scripture is a beautiful and rare treasure all on its own!

When I think of Emma receiving this revelation I can't help but wonder if she was asking the question: "What does God expect of me?" Regardless of whether those were her exact words isn't important. What is important is section 25 is proof that God gives us direction. Just as the Lord showed Nephi how to build a ship so he could cross the sea to the promise land, the Lord showed Emma what she was to do.

If the Lord were to give you a personal revelation, what would you want it to say? I'd want it to affirm that the Lord knew who I was, that I was important, and that I was loved. I'd also want it to comfort me in my trials and encourage me in my weaknesses. Well, guess what? The Lord did all of these things for Emma in section 25. And although the Lord gave Emma this revelation, through it he revealed his will for each and every daughter of God (D&C 25:1). In verse sixteen the Lord said, "This is my voice unto *all*" (D&C 25:16, emphasis added). It is for me, you, and every other person, male, female, young, and old. Section 25 *is* for *all* of us. It is meant to fortify us, strengthen us, and give us something to hang on to amidst the challenges of life.

PRINCIPLES OF OBEDIENCE

The chapter summary in Doctrine and Covenants 25 refers to the section's teachings as "Principles of Obedience." We are taught in this section that if we follow these Principles of Obedience we will receive an eternal inheritance (D&C 25:2). Each principle is meaty enough to be pondered and studied all on its own. From hearkening unto the Lord's voice, to laying aside the things of the world, to keeping commandments continually—these profound principles guide and direct us in the ways of the Lord. Here is a listing of the Principles of Obedience taught in Doctrine and Covenants 25. Take a moment and look them over.

Principles of Obedience

- Hearken unto the voice of the Lord (verse 1)
- Be faithful and walk in the paths of virtue (verse 2)

- Behold, thy sins are forgiven thee (verse 3)
- Thou art an elect lady (verse 3)
- Murmur not because of things thou hast not seen (verse 4)
- Thy calling shall be for a comfort unto my servant[s] with consoling words, in the spirit of meekness (verse 9)
- Thou shalt expound scripture and exhort the church according to my spirit (verse 7)
- Thou shalt receive the Holy Ghost (verse 8)
- Thy time shall be given to writing and learning much (verse 8)
- Thou needest not fear (verse 9)
- Thou shalt lay aside the things of the world and seek for the things of a better (verse 10)
- Make a selection of sacred hymns (verse 11)
- Lift up thy head and rejoice (verse 13)
- Cleave unto the covenants which thou hast made (verse 13)
- Continue in the spirit of meekness; beware of pride (verse 14)
- Let thy soul delight in thy husband (verse 14)
- Keep my commandments continually (verse 15)

Over a few months, I took each of these principles one by one and thought about how I could incorporate them into my daily life. I knew I would become a better person if these attributes became part of my being— part of my every day. So for a period of time, I worked on one principle and then moved on to the next principle. And I will continue to do so the rest of my life. These principles will help you too as you journey to discover what God expects of you. Study section 25; commit to living each principle more fully. See what a difference these pathways can make in your life. You'll feel better about yourself if you do, and surprisingly you'll even feel more beautiful. As President Hinckley stated: "Of all the creations of the Almighty there is none more beautiful, none more inspiring than a lovely daughter of God who walks in [paths of] virtue with an understanding of why she should do so."[3] Why should we walk in the paths of virtue? It's as simple as this: because the Lord commanded us to do so.

NOTES

1. Gordon B. Hinckley, "If Thou Art Faithful," *Ensign*, Nov. 1984, 89.
2. Ibid.
3. Hinckley, "Words of the Prophet: Daughters of the Almighty."

4
For Such a Time as This

GOD HAS CHOSEN US OUT OF THE WORLD AND HAS GIVEN US A GREAT
MISSION. I DO NOT ENTERTAIN A DOUBT MYSELF BUT THAT WE WERE SELECTED AND
FOREORDAINED FOR THE MISSION BEFORE THE WORLD WAS.

—George Q. Cannon[1]

Have you ever questioned the power of a virtuous woman's reach? Have you ever wondered if a virtuous woman can help "stem the tide of evil"? We are living in trying times. From prophets of old to the prophets and apostles of today, we are taught that we were born for such a time as this! President Ezra Taft Benson said much is expected of us because this is our time.

> For nearly six thousand years, God has held you in reserve to make your appearance in the final days before the Second Coming of the Lord. Every previous gospel dispensation has drifted into apostasy but ours will not. . . . God has saved for the final inning some of his strongest children, who will help bear off the Kingdom triumphantly. And that is where you come in. . . . All through the ages the prophets have looked down through the corridors of time to our day. Billions of the deceased and those yet to be born have their eyes on us. Make no mistake about it. . . . There has never been more expected of the faithful in such a short period of time as there is of us.[2]

We are the faithful. *We* are the women of virtue. *We* are the women God intended for such a time as this! *We* were among the noble and great ones in the council in heaven. *We* were assigned to come to earth during this, the last dispensation before the Lord comes again. Heavenly Father saved strong, valiant, and determined spirits to live at this time because He knew he could depend on us. And we are told there will be many who will follow after us who are even greater than we are!

At Women's Conference 2007, Wendy Watson Nelson remarked: "We are here in mortality now, because we're supposed to be here, now! The doctrine is clear on this point. And among those things we are to do while we're here on earth is to complete the mortal assignments we were given premortally and to which we agreed. The Savior said that He came to earth to do the will of our Father, that same Father, who sent us."[3]

Bishop H. Burke Peterson said: "There are things for each of you to do that no one else can do as well as you. . . . If you will let Him, I testify that our Father in Heaven will walk with you through the journey of life and inspire you to know your special purpose here."[4] In 1979, President Spencer W. Kimball prophesied about our mission: "Much of the major growth that is coming to the Church in the last days will come because many of the good women (in whom there is often such an inner sense of spirituality) will be drawn to the Church in large numbers. This will happen to the degree that the women of the Church reflect righteousness and articulateness in their lives."[5] Sisters, we know *this* is truly *our* time. Our purpose is great. We have a work *only we* can accomplish. But we have to do it living as virtuous women of God and not as women of the world.

Living prophets testify, over and over, that *divinity* exists within us. But how many times have we heard this? And a better question may be, "How many times do we *have* to hear this before we truly believe it—before it *changes* how we see ourselves?" It changed how a Book of Mormon king named King Lamoni saw himself. Ammon, one of the sons of Mosiah, taught King Lamoni that he was a child of God.

> And Ammon said unto [King Lamoni]: The heavens is a place where God dwells and all his holy angels.
>
> And king Lamoni said: Is it above the earth?
>
> And Ammon said: Yea, and he looketh down upon all the children of men; and he knows all the thoughts and intents of the heart; for by his hand were they all created from the beginning.
>
> And king Lamoni said: I believe all these things which thou hast spoken. Art thou sent from God?
>
> Ammon said unto him: I am a man; and man in the beginning was created after the image of God, and I am called by his Holy Spirit

to teach these things unto this people, that they may be brought to a knowledge of that which is just and true;

And a portion of that Spirit dwelleth in me, which giveth me knowledge, and also power according to my faith and desires which are in God (Alma 18:30–35).

King Lamoni believed Ammon. He believed God knew who he was. He believed a "portion" of God's spirit was within him and he allowed this knowledge to change him. He was willing to give away all of His sins just to know God. So I ask. What are *you* willing to give up to know God? Are you willing to champion the cause of virtue?

CHAMPIONS OF VIRTUE

Although virtue has been part of our makeup since the beginning of time, *now,* more than any other time in history, women are ideally positioned to *champion* virtue! Think about it. Rights and privileges our predecessors were once denied in centuries past are now ours! We have the power to be influences for good! One hundred years ago women could not even own property and, in the year 2008, we just witnessed the first woman to run for President of the United States. Our privileges for influence are endless! Historically, women have come a long way. But as we are told, with privilege and opportunity comes responsibility.

Elder Holland said this is a "time to be grateful and optimistic." We have come to earth at the "most blessed, the most abundant and glorious time in the history of the world. . . . We have more blessings spread among more people in more parts of the world than ever before in the story of the human family."[6] We must embrace our privileges and opportunities while at the same time guarding what we know to be most precious. And what do we know? We *know* we have the fulness and restored gospel of Jesus Christ. We *know* the holy Priesthood of God has been restored to the earth. We *know* living prophets and apostles lead and guide the Church. We *know* where much is given much is required. We *know* our grandchildren, their children, and their children's children are counting on us to stay true to the gospel of Jesus Christ. They are expecting us to show them the right way. Therefore, we *know* we must be all that God created us to be. In the words of Harold B. Lee, "To be what God intended you to be . . . depends on the way you think, believe, live, dress, and conduct yourselves as true examples of Latter-day Saint womanhood, examples of that for which you were created and made."[7] We should rejoice in our opportunities.

LIVING IN CHALLENGING TIMES

What makes it challenging to live in such a time as this? President Gordon B. Hinckley stated: "No one need tell you that we are living in a very difficult season in the history of the world. Standards are dropping everywhere. Nothing seems to be sacred any more. . . . I do not know that things were worse in the times of Sodom and Gomorrah."[8] This is a difficult season—especially for women, young and old. The scriptures tell us there will come a day when evil will be called good and good evil (2 Nephi 15: 20). We are living in that day. Satan is looking for opportunities to distract women from what is most important. He knows his success in influencing future generations rests in his ability to influence the ones who *currently* have the most influence—women—*us!* If we are going to have a lasting influence for good on generations to come (whether that be our house or the White House), our quest must be to create a virtuous legacy. We must be willing to create virtuous change.

STANDING UP AND LEADING FOR THE GREATER GOOD

Mahatma Gandhi said: "You be the change you want to see in the world."[9] To bring about virtuous change, we must be the change we desire. Virtuous change begins within the sanctuaries of our own minds. Once it blossoms within our hearts, it is nurtured within the walls of our own homes and carried out into our neighborhoods and communities, even reaching out into the four corners of the earth. Sisters, our world needs the influence of virtuous women just as flowers need the sun! This is our time to stand up and lead as the virtuous women God intended us to be. It is time to take advantage of our rights and privileges and stand up for truth and righteousness. This is our time to lead!

Women walking in paths of virtue understand two things: (1) The time to stand up and lead is NOW! And (2) making choices always must be based on the greater good. The stories of Esther and Ruth help illustrate these two principles. Both of these women displayed their virtuous character in two brilliant moments in time.

First, think about Esther. She was faced with a daunting challenge, but through a small and simple choice her decision determined her destiny and the destiny of a nation. Esther was a queen. She was the wife of King Ahasuerus ruling over a royal kingdom. A wicked prince had made an awful decree condemning the Jews to death. Hearing of this troubling news, Esther's guardian and cousin, Mordecai, begged and pled with

Esther to use her influence with her husband to save the Jewish people. Mordecai cried out to Esther, "Esther, you must do this! For you have come to earth for such a time as this!" (Esther 4). Esther knew who she was. She knew what she had to do. It was her time to stand up and lead.

Now, something Esther *didn't* know was how the king, her husband, would respond to her plea. And making it a little more complicated was this fact: Esther was Jewish. We don't know from scriptural accounts if the King already knew that. So, in choosing to stay true to her identity as a Jew, Esther could have been risking her own life. Still, she decided to head the call—even if it cost her the kingdom. Her time to be true to the virtue of who she was . . . was *now!* The fate of her people depended upon her.

Esther's decision saved her people. Her courageous choice "create[d] a stronger, more spiritually minded woman."[10] Esther didn't know ahead of time the outcome of her choices. She only knew she had to be true to her identity, and she knew she had to stand up and lead. She believed the wise words of Mordecai that she indeed had come to earth "for such a time"!

Just like Esther, we don't know the consequences of our decisions ten, twenty, thirty, or a hundred years down the road. What we do know is our decisions will have an impact—whether it will be for good or bad. Our decisions *do* matter. Even the small and simple ones. "Out of small things proceedeth that which is great" (D&C 64:33). Our choices affect our own lives, the lives of those around us, and even those who will follow after us once our life on this earth is over.

Like Esther, we have a divine destiny. Our small and simple decisions will influence generations who *have* come and who *will* come to this earth. Like Esther, we must "excel in our purpose," stand up for virtue, and do what is right because it is the right thing to do . . . because of who we are . . . because of what we know! Because this is our time!

Now, let's consider the story of Ruth. She was a virtuous woman who focused on the greater good of others, even under difficult circumstances. Ruth's husband had passed away, and so did Orpah's, Ruth's sister-in-law. Widowed at a young age, both of these women were left to take care of themselves and their mother-in-law, Naomi. Naomi was also a widow, and without sons to care for her, she had no where to go. She encouraged Ruth and Orpah to return to their families, knowing their lives would be much easier if they did so.

I imagine Naomi saying, "I am old, Ruth. You are young! Go! Go

begin a new future. Don't worry about me, an old woman. I'll be fine."
When Ruth and Orpah heard Naomi say this, the three of them wept;
Orpah then kissed her mother-in-law and said good-bye. But Ruth chose
to stay. The scriptures say, "Ruth *clave* unto [Naomi]" (Ruth 1:14, emphasis added).

Naomi did not ask for this type of devotion. But Ruth, being a woman
of integrity and virtuous character, could not leave her mother-in-law, for
she loved her. Ruth not only chose to stay with Naomi, but wholeheart-
edly committed herself to Naomi and Naomi's religion, saying, "Intreat
me not to leave thee . . . for whither thou goest, I will go; and where thou
lodgest, I will lodge: thy people shall be my people, and thy God my
God" (Ruth 1:16). In making her decision, Ruth "relinquished the tradi-
tions of her own Moabite people in favor of the truths of Israel's God."[11]

Many years later, Ruth had a great grandson named David (the boy
who fought Goliath and who later became king of Israel), and through his
posterity (the House of David), the Savior and Lord Jesus Christ would
come (Jeremiah 23:5).[12] Did Ruth know the consequences of her decision
at the time she chose to stay with Naomi and follow Israel's' God. No.
But what she did know was the importance of basing her decision on the
greater good.

Eve, Mary, Emma, Sariah, Ruth and Esther, and other women in the
scriptures, chose the greater good. What would have happened if Mother
Eve failed to follow the plan of happiness by saying there was too much
disappointment and too much sacrifice to warrant her leaving Eden?
What would have happened if Mary, the Mother of Jesus, lacked the faith
to accept her calling as the Lord's handmaiden? What would have happened to Nephi if Sariah refused to follow Lehi into the wilderness? What
would have happened if Emma had chosen to give up on Joseph, forcing
him to endure his trials alone? These are great women who, through small
and simple choices, brought great things to pass for the greater good of
some of Heavenly Father's elect children.

Think about how modern-day sisters might apply these two principles
in their lives: Standing up for marriage, family, and motherhood. Helping
a loved one overcome an addiction. Exercising patience with a less-active
family member. Being an example of "unceasing virtue" among peers
who may not be making virtuous choices. Accepting a calling despite
feelings of inadequacy. Living within one's financial means. Saving for
a son's or daughter's mission. Practicing the principles of food storage.

Generously giving to the Church's humanitarian funds. Placing family members needs above one's own. Increasing temple attendance in spite of challenging schedules. Improving relationships with loved ones. Focusing on virtuous beauty and the "weightier matters of God."

Remember, greatness did not end with Ester and Ruth. Many more women just like them are not mentioned in the holy scriptures or upon the pages of Church history. These women have fulfilled and many more will fulfill their earthly missions with greatness. Through small and simple choices they stand up and lead for the greater good. I've been lucky enough to know great women. I'm sure you know some, too. (Don't forget . . . you're one of them!)

The Lord Knows Where to Find Virtuous Women

About ten years ago, I was attending a Young Women's broadcast at the Conference Center in downtown Salt Lake City. As I began looking around at thousands of the women and young women filling the seats inside the center (it holds about 21,000 people), I began feeling very insignificant. "Do I really matter?" I thought glancing around at all the beautiful faces. How could the Lord possibly know me, Jodi Robinson? Do I really have a significant part in the plan? A little voice inside me answered, "Jodi, there are more than three million people living in the city of Bagdad, Iraq, alone. That is one city. Think of all the people that live on this earth, in every country from China to Fiji, and here you are sitting in the Conference Center listening to a prophet of God speak. You have been given much, and where much is given much is required. The Lord knows where to find you. He knows your character. Do not doubt you are where He wants you to be." My heart filled with joy! I received a powerful, personal revelation—one that I will never forget.

All over the world, women are seeking to be virtuous. From Ghana, Africa, to Billings, Montana. From Paris, France, to Perth, Australia, women are seeking to walk in the paths of virtue. We can take comfort in knowing the Lord knows where to find them. And He knows where to find you.

He knew how to find one woman named Tauta who lives Albania (a small country next to Greece and Turkey). Tauta came to visit the United States when my sister, who was living overseas, came for a visit. Tauta's family joined the Church and was sealed in the Frankfurt Germany Temple in 2001. It had been six years since Tauta's sealing, and she was anxious to return to the temple. On a beautiful fall day, I took Tauta to the temple. Just as we stepped inside the main doors, a woman called out, "Tauta!" I couldn't believe it. I thought I was hearing things. Tauta did too. Would you believe a sister who had served a mission in Albania recognized Tauta? The timing was uncanny! I watched their tender embrace. In their loving exchange, I witnessed the care and concern these two sweet sisters had for one another. I thought to myself, "What are the odds? Two good women—one from clear across the world—and they run into each other in the temple."

Does the Lord know where to find the Tautas of the world. Yes! I know he does. He knows where to find good and virtuous women who are willing to do the Lord's work. For some, a virtuous refuge may only exist deep in their heart and mind, but nevertheless, wherever daughters of God live, whatever their circumstances, God will bless them if they will seek out virtuous places. For if they do, the Lord will always know where to find them.

STAND UP AND LEAD

If ever there were a need for virtuous women to stand up and lead in behalf of virtue, it is now! We have so much good to do in our homes, our wards, our stakes, our neighborhoods, our communities—our world. We are needed to be instruments in the Lord's hands. We are needed to help build up the kingdom of God on earth. We are needed to bring souls unto Christ. We are needed to lift up one another and to bear one another's burdens. If you're thinking you're too young, think again. Joan of Arc was a most memorable young woman in history, who was steadfast and immovable in the cause of Christ. In a famous play by Maxwell Anderson, she exclaimed, "One life is all we have to live, and we live it as we believe in living it, and then it's gone. But to surrender what you are, and live without belief—that's more terrible than dying—more terrible than dying young." Joan of Arc was burned at the stake for her beliefs. She was just 16.[13]

If you are thinking you are too old, think of Mother Teresa. She spent her whole life devoted to the cause of uplifting the poor and loving the unlovable. She had no professional training. She had no fancy title. She didn't even have money. Yet her influence and example affected the entire world. Her humble philosophy was, "If you can't feed a hundred people, then feed just one."[14]

If you're thinking you're not good enough . . . how are you defining *good enough*?

The truth is we are more than good enough. We are daughters of a Heavenly Father and, on that belief alone, we are enough and more! We may not be Esther. We may not be Ruth, or Mary, or Eve. We don't have to be. I am me. And you are you. That was good enough for Heavenly Father when He created us, and it should be good enough for us here and now.

WHERE AND HOW DO I LEAD?

The Lord needs Esthers and Ruths, but he also needs Jodis, Emilys, Isabelles, and Rebeccas. He needs Ieeshas, Yasukos, and Kianas as well as Rosios, Angelas, and Carmens. He needs our talents! He needs our vision! If you're asking how can I lead? Where can I lead? What can I do to lead? Just look around you. You'll find many places where your virtuous example is needed. You are needed in your immediate family to teach the importance of scripture study, family prayer, service, and temple worthiness. You are needed in your extended family to build loving relationships that echo the truths of the eternal plan of happiness. You are needed to help carry the burdens of your neighbors. You are needed in your ward and stake to be an example of virtue to our young women. You are needed in your community to stand up for values important to the Lord. You are needed in a world that suffers from sin. Your hands can reach down and lift up those lonely souls who have lost their way. Grab on to "one of the least of these" and lead them to God. Ladies, there is work to be done!

As mothers, our first priority is, of course, to our own families. We must not discount the virtuous example for good that we can be within our own homes and among our own family. As mothers we are nurturing virtuous character in our little ones each and every day. We hold the power to raise virtuous sons and daughters unto the Lord by teaching them what women should look like, dress like, and act like. We must stay true to who we are so our children will stay true to who they are. If you are not yet a mother, please do not discount the good you can do within your sphere of influence. Think of the wonderful influence you can have as you develop strong relationships of trust with those in your family and extended family. Remember "all things must come to pass in their time" and you are "laying the foundation of a great work" (D&C 64:32–33). No matter if you are young, old, married, single, tall, short, blonde, brunette, whoever you are, and wherever you live, it doesn't matter. The Lord loves you. He needs you to help bring about virtuous change.

President Jeffrey Holland has stated:

> For the privilege of living in such a time [we] have a responsibility that has never come in exactly this way to any other dispensation of Church members. *We* are the people in the eternal scheme of things who must prepare the Church of the Lamb for the arrival of the Lamb. No earlier people in any ancient day ever had that assignment. What a tremendous responsibility! This means that before this is over we have to look like His Church members would look and act like His Church members would act. This will require all of us to move closer and closer to the heart of the gospel, to true principles of discipleship and faith, qualities of the heart and spirit. In short it means we have to live and be, to actually demonstrate what it is we are always so quick to say that we "know" in our testimony meetings.[15]

We owe it to our posterity to live up to our eternal potential to come out of the world and lay up our treasures in heaven. We owe it to God to seek out a better way.

THANK YOU FOR KNOWING THERE IS A BETTER WAY

President Gordon B. Hinckley said: "I cannot say enough of appreciation for your determination to live by the standards of the Church, to walk with the strength of virtue. . . . Thank you for knowing there is a better way. Thank you for the will to say no. Thank you for the strength to deny temptation and look beyond and above to the shining light of your eternal potential."[16] Sisters, let us find our greatest strength in virtue. Let us choose the better part.

WHAT ARE YOU DOING WITH YOUR NOW

What is going on in your life right now? Are you a busy mother raising children? Are you finishing school? Are you single and wondering what life has in store for you? Are you moving on to a new phase in your career or experiencing the empty nest for the first time? Are you contemplating the contributions you can make in this world?

Please know that no matter where you are on life's stage, no matter what is happening in your life, you have something in common with millions of faithful women all over the world: *you* (and I, and they) have been sent to this earth "for such a time as this" (Esther 4). So I ask: What are you doing with your *now?* Who are you becoming? Are you focusing on what is most important? Are you staying true to who you are so when Lord calls on you He can use you as a proper instrument in his kingdom? Whether that means raising a family, performing missionary work, serving in church callings, or whatever your *call* may be . . . will he know where to find you? Will the Lord find you doing the work of a virtuous woman for such a time as this?

Notes

1. Comp. Jerreld L. Newquist, *Gospel Truth* (Salt Lake City: Zions Bookstore, 1957), 1:22.

2. Ezra Taft Benson, "In His Steps," *Speeches of the Year 1979* (Provo, Utah: Brigham Young University Press, 1980), 59.

3. Nelson, "For Such a Time as This."

4. H. Burke Peterson, "Your Life Has a Purpose," *New Era*, May 1979, 4.

5. Spencer W. Kimball, "The Role of Righteous Women," *Ensign*, Nov. 1979, 102.

6. Jeffrey R. Holland and Patricia Holland, "What Time is This?" BYU Women's Conference, May 4, 2007.

7. Harold B. Lee, "Maintain Your Place As a Woman," *Ensign,* Feb. 1972, 48.

8. Gordon B. Hinckley, as quoted in Quentin L. Cook, "Strengthen Faith as You Seek Knowledge," *New Era*, Sep. 2008, 2.

9. The Quotations Page, "Classic Quotes," http://www.quotationspage.com/quote/27184.html.

10. Kathleen H. Hughes, "Lessons from the Old Testament: Coming of Age," *Ensign*, Dec. 2006, 37.

11. Michael Wilcox, *Daughters of God* (Salt Lake City: Deseret Book, 1998), 87.

12. *Primary 6: Old Testament,* 114.

13. Beverly Campbell, "Challenges of the 80s," *New Era*, Apr. 1981, 18.

14. Quotationsbook, "Mother Teresa's Quotes," http://quotationsbook.com/quote/36000/.

15. Holland and Holland, "What Time is This?"

16. Gordon B. Hinckley, "Stand Strong against the Wiles of the World," *Ensign*, Nov. 1995, 98.

5

In the World But Not of the World

LOVE NOT THE WORLD, NEITHER THE THINGS
THAT ARE IN THE WORLD. IF ANY [WOMAN] LOVE THE WORLD,
THE LOVE OF THE FATHER IS NOT IN [HER].
—1 John 2:15

As long, summer days drew near at the end of my ninth grade year, I spent hours lying on the grass in my backyard, daydreaming about what life was going to be like in the few short years ahead. As I attended my Sunday meetings, seminary classes, and mutual activities, I could feel my testimony growing. I had begun to plant my feet firmly in gospel soil (thanks to goodly parents). I looked toward to my future with great anticipation, but, like all teenagers, my life was not without challenges.

One blue-sky Saturday afternoon, my parents called a family meeting. "Kids, your dad has some exciting news," my mother informed us. (I was *so* hoping my parents were going to take us to Disneyland.) Mom continued. "Dad has accepted a new job in another sate. We get to have a family adventure! A new house! A new school! It will be so much fun!" My eleven-year-old brother cheered; my eight-year-old sister clapped her hands; and I let out a gut-wrenching sob, "Noooooo!"

"I'm not moving!" I exclaimed as I ran up stairs to my bedroom and flung myself on my bed. Moving sounded as much fun as riding a roller coaster without a seat belt.

Leave behind my friends, my school, everything I had known since I was nine? What were my parents thinking? An adventure? You've got to be kid-ding! I saw none of this as being advantageous to my future plans. All I could see was frightening, new change.

Well, weeks later, the moving truck showed up in the driveway. I realized my hunger strike wasn't working nor were my threats to move in with my friend Amy down the street. Our family *was* moving, and there was nothing I could do about it.

"Illinois, here we come!" my Dad said excitedly as he steered the motor home out of the driveway and down the street. Good-bye Rockwell drive and hello corn fields? No mountains? Early morning seminary? Life as I knew it was over.

Long story short, we arrived at our new home three weeks before school was to start. I met a girl my first Sunday at Church. She informed me that only one boy at my high school was a member of the Church. Among twelve hundred students, I was going to be the *only* Mormon girl. That meant not very many (if any) students would know what a Mor-mon's standards were unless I chose to live them. No one would know that I believed in the Word of Wisdom unless I chose not to drink. No one would know I believed in chastity before marriage unless I chose to be chaste. The bottom line was no one would know what I believed unless I lived the standards of the Church. That was easy to do where I had come from. Most of my friends, even non-members, all had the same standards. There wasn't a question about what was "okay" and what wasn't. We all just knew.

My first social experience at my new school was a non-date dance held at the end of the first week. They called it a "stomp." Some girls in my P.E. class invited me to meet them there. I accepted their invita-tion, thinking it would be a good place to meet some other new friends. As my mom pulled into the parking lot, I could hear the rumblings of loud music coming from the gymnasium. Getting out of the backseat, I mumbled, "Here goes nothing."

"Have fun!" Mother encouraged. She waved at me and blew me a kiss.

I quickly found the girls I knew. We started talking and then started dancing. At first I was having a good time, but as the night wore on I realized many of the kids had been drinking—including the girls I was with. I didn't feel so good about being there, so after a short while, I left the gym, found a pay phone, and called home.

"Mom, you need me to come and get me."

"Really? You've only been there an hour," my mom said curiously. When I told her what had happened and that I felt really uncomfortable, she said, "Oh, I'll be right there."

The next Monday the girls asked me what happened to me. I told them straightforwardly that I had gone home because I wasn't having a good time. "Oh, you don't drink," Mary said somewhat intrigued.

"No, I don't. You see I'm Mormon and we believe in this thing called the Word of Wisdom . . ."

Now, the story doesn't turn out to have one of those grand missionary moments where the girls end up begging me to take them to Church and have the missionary discussions. Nothing like that. But what did happen was this: through this experience, and many others that soon followed, I learned what living in the world but not being of the world really meant. You see, that was the seminary theme that year. And thank goodness it stuck in my mind like glue! I thought about it every day. "Being in the world but not of the world." It was my lifeline. And still today I am forever grateful for those nine, little words that kept ringing in my ears, hour after hour, dance after dance, month after month, all through my high school years. They gave me courage to stand up for what I believed in.

Now, more than two decades later, you could say I graduated from seminary and am required to live this principle at a Master's degree level. I now know that "living *in* the world but not being *of* the world" teaches a **higher law**, and it is this: Heavenly Father expects His daughters not only to *not* be worldly, but to be so far removed from the world that they practice holiness and purity continually (D&C 46:33). *But how do we do this when we live IN the world*—a world that is not so pure and not so holy?

LOVE NOT THE WORLD

First, we learn not to love the world. "Whosoever therefore will be a friend of the world is the enemy of God" (James 4:4). "Love not the world, neither the things that are in the world. If any [woman] love the world, the love of the Father is not in [her]" (1 John 2:15). The scriptures teach us the world is not God's friend and the world is not our friend. If we desire to be virtuous women of God, we must not befriend the world, nor can we love the things that are in it.

Now, before we get too far, let me throw out a caution here as I'm referring to this thing called "the world." You see there is a tendency for us to point the finger at others and say, "Oh, yes! We know. That darn world out *there*!" as if it is a far away place that exists somewhere else, somewhere outside of our own homes, somewhere other than our own neighborhoods, and surely somewhere outside of our own beings.

"It's the Joneses down the street who live in the world, not me."

"I attend *most* of my Church meetings."

"I only wear it when I'm on vacation."

"It's not like I'm doing it for the wrong reasons."

The truth be told, the world *is* among us—and, in some ways, it is even inside us.

HOLD BACK BABYLON

President Gordon B. Hinckley said: "The world is constantly crowding in on us. From all sides we feel the pressure to soften our stance, to give in here a little and there a little. . . . We must stand firm. We must hold back the world."[1] Can you feel the world crowding in a little here and a little there? Do you feel the pressure to soften your stance on things you know you shouldn't? Every day, on every street, in every house, this question is being asked by someone, "Should I just lower my standards a little? Wouldn't it be easier if I did?" Everywhere we turn, we are being asked to give in a little here and a little there. We're encouraged to loosen our stance in the name of social progress, acceptance, and tolerance. But as President Hinckley taught, we must stand firm and hold back Babylon.

Babylon was a city destroyed because of wickedness. Listen to the description of people who lived in that city: "They seek not the Lord to establish his righteousness, but every [woman] walketh in [her] own way, and after the image of [her] own god, whose image is in the likeness of the world, and whose substance is that of an idol, which waxeth old and shall perish in Babylon, even Babylon the great, which shall fall" (D&C 1:16). To hold back Babylon, we must not settle for lesser things. We must not walk in our own way seeking worldly pursuits, pleasures, and distractions. Instead, we must choose to walk in the Lord's way and seek after the image of God.

RETREAT FROM THE EDGE

As a youth in the Young Women organization, I once heard a story about a king who was trying to choose a kingsman to someday rule over his kingdom. The king decided he would hold a contest. The king gave two men a challenge: each man would take a turn driving the king's chariot up a steep, winding, and mountainous road. Whoever could prove he was the best chariot driver would become the king's heir.

The first man decided to show the king his driving savvy by ripping around the sharp corners, proving he could come within inches of the cliff's edge without falling off. With great agility, he was able to maintain his balance. The second driver, however, decided to take a different approach. From the beginning, he chose to drive much more cautiously than the first. He slowed down around the quick curves. He pulled away from the edge, never even getting close to it. It took him a lot longer than the first contestant to reach the top of the mountain. The villagers wondered if he had made a wise decision.

The contest ended and the two drivers approached the king. The king then asked the second driver why he stayed so far away from the edge of the cliff. The man replied: "Sir, knowing that even the best of drivers make mistakes, I wanted to stay as far away from the edge as possible. As your chariot driver I would be responsible for your safety and wouldn't want to risk your life, or my own life, in an act of carelessness."

When it came time to choose the winner of the race, is it surprising that the king chose the second driver? The king knew the driver who kept his distance from the edge would always strive to keep him and his family safe from danger.

At times, the edge may not be as far away as we think. Elaine S. Dalton, Young Women General President, stated: "Sometimes we think we can live on the edge and still maintain our virtue. But that is a risky place to be."[2] We lose our virtue when we get even a little "too close" to the edge. When we step out of the light—even if it is for a second—we step into darkness. In quoting C. S. Lewis, James E. Faust stated in his Presidency address in the January 2007 *Ensign*, "[Satan's] cumulative effect is to edge the man away from the Light and out into the Nothing. . . . Indeed, the safest road to Hell is the gradual one."[3] To enjoy the blessings of the light, we must retreat from the edge. Actually, we must "stay in the middle of the straight and narrow path."[4] Truth be told, Satan knows that for women of God, the edge is simply a place where many of us dare not go. He knows we won't end up in some bar trying to "hook up" or surf the Internet for a cyberspace connection. We're far too sophisticated for that. And Satan knows this. So what does he do instead? He pushes us to the edge in more subtle ways. He entices us to dabble in fashion that is considered to be "worldly." *"It's just a T-shirt,"* he rationalizes.

He entices us with magazines, books, Internet sites, and television shows that glamorize sexuality and tolerate immorality. *"It's just a TV show."* He encourages us to spend time large blocks of time being preoccupied with our physical appearance. *"It's your body. You deserve to do whatever you want to it."* He intrigues us with glamour, idealizes social status, and, on important matters of virtue he encourages us to remain "neutral." *"People will think you're judgmental if you take a stand. You wouldn't want that to happen, now would you?"*

Ladies! Why is it that we refuse to go over the edge, yet, find it "okay" to get close enough to look over it? Elder Larry Gibbons of the Seventy says, "We cannot keep one foot in the Church and one foot in the world."[5] Those who desire to not be "of the world" will wisely heed his counsel: "Don't drift; don't wander; don't dabble; be careful. Remember, [we can] not flirt with evil. Stay out of the devil's territory. Do not give Satan any home-field advantage."[6] In other words, *stay far away from the edge.* Remember, *stay in the middle of the straight and narrow path.* Remember, to leave the light, all we have to do is take one step into the dark. The thing we must do is ask ourselves each and every day: Am I drifting? Am I dabbling? Am I wandering? Am I flirting a little with the things of the world? Am I giving any home-field advantage to the adversary? Sisters, to hold back Babylon, we must know how to live *in* the world but not be *of* the world. And we must do it faithfully each and every day.

UNDERSTAND THE LAW OF OPPOSITION

In the world, there is opposition. It was intended to be that way. Opposition is part of life. It's actually a necessary part of God's plan of happiness. The scriptures teach us there must be opposition in all things (2 Nephi 2:11). "Wherefore, man could not act for himself save it should be that he was enticed by the one or the other" (2 Nephi 2:16). Opposition is for our "profit and learning" (2 Nephi 2:14). "But behold, all things have been done in wisdom of [God] who knoweth all things. Adam fell that men might be; and men are, that they might have joy" (2 Nephi 2:24–25).

THERE IS NO NEUTRAL ZONE

One popular philosophy that Satan masterfully teaches is that there is such a thing as the "Neutral Zone." But, *neutral* was never part of God's plan. In the garden of Eden, Heavenly Father did not give Adam and Eve the tree of "neutral." He gave them the tree of knowledge of good and evil—two exact opposites (Moses 3:9). When Father in Heaven was explaining the commandments to our first parents, he didn't say, "Oh, and by the way, don't worry about the 'neutral' areas. You can't get into too much trouble if you stay within the 'neutral zone.' " No! He said, "Covenant with me, follow my Beloved Son, and he will teach you that my ways are not the world's ways." In matters of virtue, we are either on a virtuous side of the road or we're not. But we're never in the "neutral zone."

THERE ARE NO SHADES OF GRAY

In addition to confusing us with his "neutral zone" philosophy, Satan confuses us by coloring his deceptions with shades of gray. But remember, to God, the gray areas are just another shade of black. There is right and wrong. Black and white. Yes and no. This is the law of opposition in *all* things. Christ said: "They who are not for me are against me" (2 Nephi 10:16). "I am the way, the truth, and the life" (John 14:6). "No man can serve two masters: for either he will hate the one, and love the other; or else he will hold to the one, and despise the other" (Matthew 6:24). We cannot serve God and mammon at the same time. The law of opposition prohibits it. "For God doth not walk in crooked paths, neither doth he turn to the right hand nor to the left, neither doth he vary from that which he hath said, therefore his paths are straight, and his course is one eternal round" (D&C 3:2). The path of virtue is not a winding road of neutral walkways and shades of gray. Virtuous paths are straight and narrow paths. They lead us in one direction—to eternal life (2 Nephi 33: 9). The bottom line is we need to be better at drawing our lines between good and evil.

The word *evil* has such a strong connotation that we sometimes hesitate to use it. Maybe we're fearful of calling it like we see it; afraid that we'll hurt feelings or offend. But if something is not good then what else is it? Not really bad? Not *so* bad that we can't "handle it"? At least for just a little while? Do you see where I'm going with this? How can we see something that is "evil" as "neutral" or a "shade of gray?" It is what it is. There is no such thing as "almost evil." An outfit isn't "almost modest." It either is or it isn't. Something isn't *almost* tight, *almost* honest, *almost* holy, *almost* pure, or *almost* virtuous. One doesn't just *almost* keep the Sabbath or *almost* pay tithing or *almost* keep the commandments. We either do or we don't. That's pretty simple math.

One could argue philosophically, that neutrals *do* exist and that shades of gray are still "safe." And, yes, I guess the Lord is not overly-concerned with whether or not we buy a can of peas or corn. And he isn't fretting over whether we buy Western Family or Dole, or whether we shop at Walmart or K-Mart. Or whether we have beige carpet or blue carpet. But in matters of virtue and moral agency, of what is right and what is wrong, Christ *is* concerned what we choose, and he is counting on us to recognize the difference between good and evil.

In God's eyes, one inch makes a difference. President George Albert Smith (1870–1951), eighth president of the Church, said: "If you cross to the devil's side of the line one inch, you are in the tempter's power, and if he is successful, you will not be able to think or even reason properly, because you will have lost the spirit of the Lord."[7]

Spencer W. Kimball stated: "Temptations are great. Satan tells us that black is white. He lies to us; therefore, we must be prepared to make a bold stand before Satan . . . and against principalities and powers and the rulers of darkness. We need the whole armor of God that we may withstand."[8]

STAY AWAY FROM SNAKES

Some of the best advice I ever received was "stay away from snakes or you'll get bit." Unfortunately it was after I had already been bitten. Why did I get bit? Simple. Because I got too close to a snake. You see, some boys in my neighborhood were carelessly handling a pet snake—a baby boa constrictor (which was not so "baby" considering ti was four feet long). Being the "save the animals" kind of gal that I am, I stepped in to try to save the snake from the treacherous hands of teenage boys.

"Hey, put that snake down!" I yelled marching toward them with conviction. It turns out I stepped too close to the boy holding the snake and the snake, rattled from too much handling, lurched out and bit the closet thing to him—my arm. *Ouch!* Here I thought I was doing that snake a favor by trying to save it. But, nonetheless, that snake bit me anyway. Perhaps, we can apply two principles of learning, using this illustration. (1) The safest place to be is far away from snakes—far away from the influence of the adversary. (2) In a world of clamoring voices, some influences seem friendly enough but in reality are still poisonous, and some even bite!

Recently, we were boating in a desert lake in eastern Utah. We anchored the boat along the sandy shoreline so the kids could build sand castles. My husband decided to hike up the desert hill just a few yards from the main shoreline, and the kids followed him. He stopped to investigate four giant holes in the sandstone. When he looked down through the top hole, he saw that the holes were all connected. So he decided to jump down into the top hole and crawl out through one of the bottom ones. Just after he jumped down into the hole, he heard a slight rattling sound. Curled up in the corner was a rattlesnake. My husband was sharing quarters with a very undesirable fellow. (Yikes!) Thankfully, he quickly got out of the hole and safely hurried the kids away from danger.

Maybe we don't look at every decision we make in life as opting to share our space with snakes. But every choice we make has a consequence and we don't choose our consequences. They choose us! (When I got bit, that snake definitely chose me!) Poor choices will bite us eventually. We may avoid negative consequences for awhile, but it is always safer (and easier in the long run) to recoil from the devil's influence like we would a poisonous snake.

BECOME HOLY

If we are going to be the virtuous women God intended us to be, more than anything, we must learn to love what is holy. James L. Ferrell said in his book, *The Holy Secret,* "If we don't enjoy holiness here, we will not have the opportunity to experience it [in the hereafter]. . . Holy days lead us to holy places, and holy places then transform our days."[9]

How exactly do we become holy? James E. Faust said: "[Holiness] comes by faith and through obedience to God's laws and ordinances. . . . [when we are holy] God then purifies the heart by faith and the heart becomes purged from that which is profane and unworthy. When holiness is achieved by conforming to God's will, one *knows intuitively* that which is wrong."[10] What a marvelous concept Elder Faust teaches. We become holy through faith and obedience and through that process, something spectacular then happens to our hearts—our hearts becomes purified! Which means our hearts desire what is holy! With a holy heart, we won't have to spend so much time fretting over what to choose because we will *instinctively know* what is holy, and we will *desire* what is holy. Best of all, we will *love* what is holy. And loving what is holy will help us become holy. Then, we will become more like God; more of whom he desires us to be. The virtues expressed in one of my favorite hymns, "More Holiness Give Me," articulate what *more* is:

More holiness give me,
More strivings within,
More patience in suff'ring,
More sorrow for sin,
More faith in my Savior,
More sense of his care,
More joy in his service,
More purpose in prayer.
More gratitude give me,
More trust in the Lord,
More pride in his glory,
More hope in his word,
More tears for his sorrows,
More pain at his grief,
More meekness in trial,
More praise for relief.
More purity give me,
More strength to o'ercome,
More freedom from earthstains,
More longing for home.
More fit for the kingdom,
More used would I be,
More blessed and holy
More, Savior, like thee.[11]

We are not missing out by "living *in* the world and not being *of* the world." I know sometimes we may think we are, but we're not. We are not left with less. In reality we have *more*—so much more of what *really* matters.

LEAVE THE WORLD BEHIND

Sometimes when we're trying to become more holy the world seems to crowd in on us even more. Have you noticed that? Just when you decide to do better, temptation seems to come on a little stronger. At such times we might wish to pack our bags and head for the wilderness just like the prophet Lehi did with his family. Let's think on this for a moment.

What if you could leave the world behind and go somewhere far away—far away from all the worldly muck? (Well, I've been in desert muck before and I readily admit that I would want to bring a few sundries such as soap, toilet paper, and a portable shower, not to mention a few packages of Hershey's kisses. I could *never* be totally without chocolate!) Life in the wilderness (desert or no desert) has some positive points. It seems simpler, easier. Much slower than life in the fast lane; however, we have to remember that we knew our purpose long before we came to live on earth. We knew entering mortality in the latter days would be fast-lane-living at its best! We were prepared to live in these times and endure in these times.

Elder Neal A. Maxwell once said, "When anciently we shouted for joy in anticipation of this mortal experience, we did not then think it would be ordinary and pedestrian at all. We sensed the impending high adventure."[12] It's an adventure all right! And right in the middle of it the women of the Church have been asked to stand up and be agents of virtuous change: "If anyone can change the dismal situation into which we are sliding, it is you. Rise up, O women of Zion, rise to the great challenge which faces you."[13] Sisters, we must answer this call and leave the world behind seeking out our own wilderness and seeking out that which is holy.

Maybe you're thinking, "Hey, I've already accepted this challenge. I'm doing what I'm supposed to be doing. I'm serving in my calling at Church. I'm holding family home evening. I'm fulfilling my visiting teaching responsibilities and lifting my neighbor's burdens from time to time. I'm not living *of* the world." And if that is the case, that is wonderful! Truly it is. But pause for just moment. Let the spirit speak to your soul. Is there anything . . . anything at all that you could be doing differently? A little better, perhaps? Considering how consuming our day-to-day adventures can be, isn't there something consuming you a little here, and little there? Is there something that just might . . . just maybe . . . be preventing you from leaving the world behind? Ask yourself: "What can I do to become more holy?" Perhaps the answer begins with a desire to live more for eternity and less for today. I believe C. S. Lewis said it best: "If you live for the next world, you get this one in the deal; but if you live only for this world, you lose them both."[14] Let go of the world and cling to what is holy.

BECOME PECULIAR, DISTINCT, AND DIFFERENT

A few years ago, the walls in my family room desperately needed painting. I had settled on painting them a neutral color. "Beige. I'll go with beige," I decided. Looking over the sea of paint chips at the hardware store, I was surprised to discover such a plethora of options. There was Oatmeal, Sand, Flesh, Natural Beige, Toffee, Coffee Cream, Wheat, Off-white, Almost Bare, and so on and so on. I had no idea that beige could be so complicated! At last, I narrowed my choices down to three. To decide which of the three chips was indeed the *right* color, I took them home to do a little test.

While standing under the light in my family room, I held up two of the paint chips to my light fixture. I was surprised to see how similar the colors looked. They just sort of blended together. In a certain light, they even looked exactly the same. The third color, however, was a shade "distinct and different" enough to set it apart from the other two colors of beige. So I made my decision to go with that one.

As women living in the Latter-days, we need not be the shade of beige that blends in with the women of the world. Rather, we need to stand apart as a "peculiar" color of virtue. Surely, you and I both know how easy it would be to be Oatmeal or Sand (and since I'm talking "worldly" it certainly would be easy to be Flesh!). But you and I have a royal lineage. We know who we are. We have been given light and knowledge of who we are and who we are destined to become. We can't just blend in! You and I, and others like us, need to stand out! We need to become a sisterhood "distinct and different" so much so that we stand apart from the women of the world.[15]

God wants us to be a peculiar people. He wants us to be an ensign to all the nations. "For thou art an holy [woman] unto the Lord thy God, and the Lord hath chosen thee to be a *peculiar* [person] unto himself, above all the nations that are upon the earth" (Deuteronomy 14:2, emphasis added). What does it mean to be "peculiar"? (If you ask my children— they'll tell you my tendency to not finish my sentences when my brain is multi-tasking and how they have to do that for me. That's what they'd say makes "Mom" peculiar. But that's not the kind of peculiar I'm talking about.) According to the Bible Dictionary, the Hebrew word *segullah*, which is translated to mean *peculiar* means exclusive or special. We are meant to be exclusive or special; a "virtuous kind of beauty" special.

At the time Spencer W. Kimball was president of the Church he pleaded with the Sisters to become a more *peculiar* group of women "to the degree that [they] are seen as *distinct and different*—in happy ways—from the women of the world."[16] Think on these two words for a moment—distinct and different. What do those words mean to you? Why did President Kimball, more than two decades ago, choose to give women this prophetic counsel? Perhaps, he knew it would become easier and easier for women of faith to just blend in with the women of the world, so he gave the "peculiar challenge" so that we would rise up and become a sisterhood of "distinct and different" enough women as to not be mistaken for being *of* the world.

How does being a peculiar shade of virtue, distinct and different, fit into our everyday lives? Ideally, *every* path we walk should be a peculiar path—a distinct and different path. Sure, it's easy to walk in a distinct path when we're going to church on Sunday, or when we're going to the temple. But what about when we're shopping at the mall, going to the gym, working in the backyard, or when we're on vacation? Hmmmm. Are we the same women in these places as we are in sacrament meeting? God is the same yesterday, today, and forever (1 Nephi 10:18), and He expects us to be a shade of virtue, peculiar, distinct and different, *all* of the time—yesterday, today, and forever.

Be Happy Living Your Not-So-Fairy-Tale Life

One final thought on "living in the world but not of the world." As little girls, we believed in fairy tales with magical kingdoms and castles. Now that we're all grown up, many of us have experienced trials and afflictions that have caused us to question our belief in the fairy tale. We think, "I must be living the 'not-so-fairy-tale' version." But that's not true. We are, in fact, living a fairy tale. We are daughters of a mighty King, who lives in a glorious kingdom, who desires for all of His daughters to someday return to Him and build kingdoms of their own with their very own princes. The happily ever after *will* someday be a reality. But, you know that "happily ever *after*"? Well, the fairy tale comes *after* everything. *After* we have endured. *After* we have passed the test. *After* we have given everything we possibly have to give.

The part of the fairy tale we're living is the "endure to the end" part. And while we're enduring we should try to be happy. Sometimes that's hard to do. Especially when the fairy tale plays out more like an adventure novel, or maybe even a fable, mystery, or comedy. (Seriously, where's the fantasy when Prince Charming isn't always so charming and the chariot you're driving is a mini-van covered in fishy-cracker crumbs.) In moments of trials and tribulations, we wonder if Cinderella ever gets to go to the ball. Guess what? She does. And she will. *If* she chooses to be true to the virtue of who she is and always has been.

As my life has progressed, I can tell you it isn't the grand castle, or the glass slippers, or the fairy godmother that makes our fairy tale a fairy tale. It is the pure knowledge that the daughter of a King is *really* a daughter of a King. And even though she is currently working hard in the scullery, she is learning valuable lessons that will some day make her worthy of her crown. (Thanks, Holly, for reminding me of this.) Let's not focus on what isn't part of our fairy tale. Let's focus on what is! And remember, every princess's fairy tale *will* have a happy ending . . . eventually. For I know without a doubt . . . eventually will eventually come.

NOTES

1. Gordon B. Hinckley, "An Ensign to the Nations, a Light to the World." *Ensign*, Nov. 2003, 82.

2. Elaine S. Dalton, "Stay on the Path," *Ensign*, May 2007, 112.

3. James E. Faust, "The Forces That Will Save Us," *Ensign*, Jan. 2007, 4.

4. Larry W. Gibbons, "Wherefore, Settle This in Your Hearts," *Ensign*, Nov. 2006, 102.

5. Ibid.

6. Ibid.

7. Joseph Smith Jr. as quoted in James E. Faust, "The Devil's Throat," *Liahona*, May 2003, 51.

8. Spencer W. Kimball, "The Blessings and Responsibilities of Womanhood," *Ensign*, Mar. 1976, 70.

9. James L. Ferrell, *The Holy Secret* (Salt Lake City: Deseret Book, 2008), 141.

10. James E. Faust, "Standing in Holy Places," *Liahona*, May 2005, 67. Emphasis added.

11. "More Holiness Give Me," *Hymns*, no. 131.

12. Neal A. Maxwell, "Grounded, Rooted, Established, and Settled," *BYU Speeches*, 15 September 1981.

13. Gordon B. Hinckley, "Walking in the Light of the Lord." *Ensign*, Nov. 1998, 97.

14. http://www.christianarsenal.com/study/Acts/Acts20v1-38.pdf

15. Kimball, "The Role of Righteous Women."

16. Ibid. Emphasis added.

6

The Virtue of God's Word

"THE WORD HAD A GREAT TENDENCY TO LEAD THE PEOPLE
TO DO THAT WHICH WAS JUST . . . THEREFORE . . .
TRY THE VIRTUE OF THE WORD OF GOD."
— Alma 31:5)

When attending college, I often visited my grandparents who lived only four blocks away from my campus apartment. Opening up their front door I'd holler, "Grandma! Grandpa! Are you home?" More often than not, I'd hear a soft, deep voice say, "Up here, Jodi." That was Grandpa calling down from his upstairs study, which overlooked the living room. Sure enough, I'd find him sitting in his favorite wooden chair, always with his scriptures opened, along with a Church magazine or two, and several inspirational books laid out across his desk. My grandfather was a religion professor at Brigham Young University for thirty years. Although he had retired from full-time teaching when I started at BYU, he taught one or two classes each semester and still studied and prepared as if he taught full-time.

Several years after I graduated, my grandfather passed away. Shortly after his passing, I was visiting with my grandmother in her dining room. The room smelled of roses, ferns, lilies, and blue carnations (blue for BYU, of course). Looking around the room, I had never seen so many flower arrangements in all my life. I then noticed something I didn't always see—Grandfather's scriptures were sitting there on the table. His scriptures were *always* upstairs in the study on his desk. I couldn't resist picking up the brown, leather quad. I ran my fingers across the golden engraving of Grandpa's name. The *e* in his last name was almost undetectable. As I opened them up I immediately noticed how worn the pages looked. Some edges of the pages were so worn that the words were faded and barely legible. Every page was covered in colorful markings and yellow sticky-notes containing Grandpa's scribbled notations. I could tell this particular set of scriptures had been well-used. As I read some of my Grandfather's markings, I realized I was reading some of his most personal thoughts.

"Every one wants to know who gets Grandpa's scriptures," said Grandma, interrupting my trance.

"Really?" I responded not putting two and two together. A second later it hit me. Of course! Who wouldn't want to have Grandpa's scriptures within their possession? As I pondered what the scriptures meant to my grandfather, it was crystal clear that they represented his lifetime legacy. Grandpa read, studied, memorized, quoted, paraphrased, and cited truths from the scriptures every day of his adult life; to his students, yes, but also to his family, and to his grandchildren and great-grandchildren. The scriptures were his legacy, not because he was a professor of religion and teaching from the scriptures was how he made his living, but because he loved them.

I want to leave my own "scripture legacy" behind for my children, grandchildren, and great-grandchildren. So, with this in mind, I spend time studying the scriptures, pondering them, marking them, and feasting on them. As I mark different verses and place sticky notes on the pages, I write down my feelings about what I read and make note if there was anything significant about it; for example, if it was answer to prayer, I write "answer to prayer" and then the date. This way it becomes a journal of sorts. Someday, when my children and grandchildren hold my leather quad in their hands, they'll know I have a deep and abiding testimony of the scriptures; they'll know I love them and live for them. Thanks, Grandpa, for leaving me your legacy of love for the virtue of God's word. You gave me a wonderful example to follow.

MORONI'S FINAL TESTIMONY AND PROMISE

My experience with my grandfather's scriptures reminds me of the last chapter in the Book of Mormon where the prophet Moroni writes his last and final testimony before he buries the plates in the Hill Cummorah. In his hands, Moroni held the scriptures, the word of God, as it was recorded by ancient prophets for hundreds of years. On those plates of gold were the words of Lehi, Alma, Abinadi, Mormon, and Helaman, as well as many other righteous leaders. Because they loved God, they recorded their testimonies of Christ in hopes to persuade others to follow Him. Moroni had the privilege of holding a scriptural legacy that spanned hundreds of years. He knew they contained precious teachings from the Lord; teachings that had the power to bring souls unto Christ—teachings that had the power to change men and women for good. Moroni writes:

> Awake, and arise from the dust . . . and put on thy beautiful gar-
> ments, O daughter of Zion; and strengthen thy stakes and enlarge thy
> borders forever, that thou mayest no more be confounded, that the
> covenants of the Eternal Father which he hath made unto thee . . . may
> be fulfilled. . . . Come unto Christ, and be perfected in him, and deny
> yourselves of all ungodliness . . . and love God with all your might,
> mind and strength, then is his grace sufficient for you, that by his grace
> ye may be perfect in Christ. (Moroni 10:31–32)

Of all the words Moroni could have chosen to seal up his testimony—he chose these. These were the words he wanted *us* to remember. He pleads with us to strengthen our stakes; come unto Christ; deny
ourselves of ungodliness; love God with all of our might, mind, and
strength; and live in such a way to claim God's mercy and grace that we
may become perfected in Christ. The scriptures will help us do all of these
things. They will help us achieve greatness and create a virtuous legacy of
our very own.

ENERGETICALLY PURSUE THE SCRIPTURES

To build a virtuous legacy, we must *try* the virtue of God's word. We
must "experiment." This means the word of God has to become more
to us than words on a page. The scriptures need to become a part of us.
They need to become who we are, what we stand for, and what we live for.
Gospel scholar Robert Millet said, "It is when the scriptures have become
ours, when they have been read and studied and memorized and quoted
and paraphrased . . . that they begin to have a transforming effect upon
our souls."[1] Spencer W. Kimball said: "If we will energetically pursue [a
study of the scriptures] in a determined and conscientious manner, we
shall indeed find answers to our problems and peace in our hearts. We
shall experience the Holy Ghost broadening our understanding, find new
insights, witness an unfolding pattern of all scripture; and the doctrines
of the Lord shall come to have more meaning to us than we ever thought

possible. As a consequence, we shall have greater wisdom with which to guide ourselves and our families."[2]

Sisters, we have to read the scriptures as if our very lives depended on them. And they do. They aren't just old stories about old people to whom we can't relate. They are about us! They were written for us in our day. You see, Nephi building a ship isn't really about Nephi. It's about you and me in our struggle to figure out how to do the impossible. The story is about having a righteous desire and finding the tools to help us accomplish our goal. It is about having faith and trusting in the Lord. Take this book for example. I didn't know how to write a book before I began. But just like Nephi asked the Lord, in faith, to show him how to build a boat, I asked the Lord to help me achieve my righteous desire, that of writing this book. I asked him to bless me with the tools to accomplish my desires. And *just* like the Lord showed Nephi how to accomplish what he needed to in order to build a ship, the Lord showed me where to find quotes and how to understand what was important in communicating my thoughts. He should me how to build my own ship.

I know with a little faith and lot of effort the stories in the scriptures can explode with personal meaning and teach with life-changing power. If we "energetically" read them daily, they will become as much a part of us as the breaths we take. But we have to give them a chance. We have to spend time reading them, pondering them, questioning them, and studying them. A casual perusal once a week, or every now and again, will not suffice.

One thing that helped me strengthen my testimony of the scriptures is having a scripture journal. I use this journal to take notes while I read. Sometimes what I write doesn't even really pertain to anything specific. But later on, as I read what I have written, I begin to see connections between what I'm reading and what I'm experiencing in my day to day life. The scriptures literally take on new meaning. They become personal. I have really enjoyed having a recording of my scripture reading. I have seen evidence of the Lord's hand guiding and directing me. This journal has brought to life the Lord's tender mercies. It has solidified my testimony of seeing the power of God in my daily life. Someday, I know it will be a wonderful gift for my children.

Something else I do to study the scriptures is to use the most recent Church magazines as study guides. Whatever scriptures are used in the articles that month I look them up, read, and study them. This helps me learn to interpret the scriptures through the eyes of some of our most trusted Church leaders. The messages in the *Ensign,* the *New Era,* and the *Friend* are inspired to teach us and to strengthen our testimonies. The topics are timely, and they really can be invaluable tools to help you understand more fully the precepts being taught in the scriptures.

TEACHERS OF GOSPEL TRUTHS

Think for a moment about what makes you and I similar to the prophet Lehi? Have you ever thought about that? Well, Lehi was a teacher. Faithful to God's commandments, he took his family into the wilderness and what did he do there? He taught his family the gospel. When you think of Lehi teaching and preaching the gospel, you may picture a large congregation. But in reality, Lehi's congregation consisted, not of tens of thousands, not even of thousands or hundreds of people. In fact, his congregation was quite small, made up of key people in his immediate and extended family: Sariah, his wife, his sons, their wives, and his grandchildren and, as time went on, his great-grandchildren. So, when we look at father Lehi in this way we see that we are *a lot* like father Lehi. We are teachers to the key people in our immediate and extended families.

Like this Book of Mormon prophet, we are responsible for teaching our own mini-congregations. As I have gathered my own children to study the scriptures, I picture Lehi and Sariah teaching their children. I picture them sitting with their family members inside their tent; the tent walls billowing in the desert wind; the sound of goats "baahing" in the background; sand beneath their sandaled feet; and little children nestled under the arms of their parents. But hold on a moment. Let's do a quick reality check because I can't say that every scripture-reading experience with my children ends with a Hallelujah chorus. (I only wish.) The truth be told, I have sent children to time-out for spitting and hitting. I have sat between children who would not stop touching each other. Once, I even sent myself to time-out because I was so frustrated I was about to cry. No, our family scripture study isn't always perfect. And sometimes I have wondered, "Is it worth it? Is anything, anything at all getting through to these kids?" But the fact is I keep at it, because mixed in with those "less-than-perfect" moments are golden moments. Like when my twelve-year-old asks me how Nephi learned to build a ship when he didn't have any blueprints. As well as my second oldest daughter reciting the whole story of Alma the younger from memory. And then of course, my favorite, when my three-year-old says, "Jesus wasn't bad-tized. He was good-tized." *These* are the moments I treasure. *These* are times I feel angels are attending me simply because I am trying to do what Jesus wants me to do. He wants me to teach my children the gospel. So, like Lehi and Sariah, I keep trying. I keep teaching. And I keep hoping and praying that the word of God will seep into my children's souls so much so that they will develop a love for the scriptures all their own.

THE FAMILY SCRIPTURE BASKET

To help my family study the scriptures, I created a Family Scripture Basket (a wonderful idea from a neighbor). In this basket are several soft-cover, blue, Book of Mormons, colored pencils, a scripture journal, and the Book of Mormon Stories (sometimes referred to as the Book of Mormon reader at the Church distribution center), and two higher-level reference books for more in-depth study. This is what we use in our family. Having everything together has made having scripture study a little easier because our scriptures are always available to us. The Scripture Basket has become a fun family tradition.

SEEK COUNSEL FROM ON HIGH TO AVOID DECEPTIONS

In addition to seeking the word of God in the scriptures, we must seek counsel from on high. This true story illustrates the importance of seeking such counsel. A group of Boy Scouts were hiking with their leaders in the primitive area of the Uintah Mountains. The group had been hiking for several hours when they came upon a shallow bend in a river. They were thirsty and stopped to fill their canteens with water. After a few minutes, the scout leader prompted the boys to move along and continue their hike since they still had several miles to go before setting up camp for the night.

After walking about one hundred yards, the scout leader stopped the group of young men, and pointed to a large figure off into the distance. A dead cow was lying in the riverbed. As they approached the lifeless body they could tell it was bloated and bloody. The leader decided to make a life lesson out of this experience, so he said to the boys, "Here is a good reason for you to remember how important it is to get as close to the 'source' as possible . . . because you never know what lies ahead up stream." He then likened this to seeking "pure" light and knowledge from above. "Always remember only the *highest* source with the *purest* information can protect us from Satan's deceptions." He was a very wise scout leader.

In matters of virtue, we have to be careful about which sources we trust. It doesn't matter if a high councilman's wife, whose sister is married to a stake president, whose niece is engaged to the son of a General Authority, whose daughter is related to the Relief Society President says something is "okay." This is *not* how we determine the "trustworthiness" of information. The only sources we can trust are the sources God trusts. There is order in God's kingdom, and God has given His trust to His prophets, apostles, and officers of His church who are set apart with divine stewardship to lead and guide the people of the Church. And, of course, any counsel given by Church leader's in stakes and wards should always be in line with God's trusted sources as previously mentioned. Following God's trusted sources provides protection against the adversary's deceptions. So where should we go for answers? Not to a sister twice removed by marriage from a cousin who said she heard it from a bishop's wife. We must go to the highest source. First, we go to the Lord. Then to his prophets and apostles, for we can *always* trust the prophets and apostles. If need be, we go to our bishop. Wise women know this. Wise women know prophets, seers, and revelators "speaketh of things as they really are, and of things as they really will be" (Jacob 4:13). Prophets and apostles "speak boldly in defense of virtue and powerfully in identifying and condemning evil. They fearlessly warn of social trends and doctrinal drifts among the people of the covenant."[3] Wise women know counsel from living prophets and apostles provides protection against the "great mists of darkness." "And it came to pass that there arose a mist of darkness; yea, even an exceedingly great mist of darkness, insomuch that they who had commenced in the path did lose their way, that they wandered off and were lost" (1 Nephi 8:23). The great mists of deception run rampant (even among faithful saints), so be very careful in whom you place your trust.

Consider this counsel from Harold B. Lee from a 1970 general conference: "We have some tight places to go before the Lord is through with this church and the world in this dispensation, which is the last dispensation. . . . The gospel was restored to prepare a people ready to receive him. . . . There will be inroads within the Church. . . . We will see those who profess membership but secretly are plotting and trying to lead the people not to follow the leadership."[4]

President Lee went on to say that we may not like what comes from the authority of the Church because it may conflict with our personal and political views or even our social life. But he counseled the saints to "listen to these things, as if from the mouth of the Lord himself, with patience and faith" and promised that if the Saints would do this "the gates of hell shall not prevail against [them] and the Lord God will disperse the powers of darkness from before [them] . . . and cause the heavens to shake for [their] good (D&C 21:6)."[5] That *was* and *still is* a powerful promise. It is an excellent reason to rely on leadership from "on high" and lean not unto our own understanding.

As we apply the virtue of the word (by studying the principles, standards, and doctrine of the Church), we will ensure we will not be deceived. "Seek counsel, and authority . . . from under [God's] hand" (D&C 122:2). "Ask, and it shall be given you; seek, and ye shall find" (Luke 11:9). The scriptures and the higher sources of truth, such as prophets and apostles, can help us in choosing right from wrong—especially when something doesn't feel inherently wrong. President James E. Faust taught that just because something "feels" okay doesn't necessarily mean it is okay. His counsel helped me set aside my emotions and listen more intently to the Holy Ghost:

> Much of what comes from the devil is alluring and enticing. It glitters and is appealing to the sensual parts of our nature. His message sounds so reasonable and easy to justify. His voice is usually smooth and intriguing. If it were harsh or discordant, nobody would listen, nobody would be enticed. Some of Satan's most appealing messages are: Everyone does it; if it doesn't hurt anybody else, it's all right; if you feel there is no harm in it, it's okay; it's the "cool" thing to do. Satan is the greatest imitator, the master deceiver, the arch counterfeiter, and the greatest forger ever in the history of the world. He comes into our lives as a thief in the night. His disguise is so perfect that it is hard to recognize him or his methods. He is a wolf in sheep's clothing. We all have an inner braking system that will stop us before we follow Satan too far down the wrong road. It is the still, small voice within us. But if we allow ourselves to succumb to Satan's tempting, the braking system begins to leak brake fluid and our stopping mechanism becomes weak and ineffective.[6]

From a distance some temptations seem "okay," "harmless," and "not a big deal." Our emotions can make it even more confusing because "feelings" can come on so strongly. What we need to do is to use our "braking system" long before we get to the stop light. The only way to know *for sure* if something is right and acceptable to God is to measure it against a Church standard. Think about what prophets have said on the matter? What does the *For the Strength of Youth* say? What do the scriptures teach? What commandment relates to what you desire? After you have sought out the standard, you use that as your measuring tool. Setting aside our emotions and using standards to help us make decisions will help us make the right decision.

Years ago, I was seeking an answer to a very personal question. I needed an answer. I desired an answer. And I wanted what I wanted so badly. My emotions were so confusing. At times I would think, "I've got my answer. I'll go forward." But then I would feel hesitant and would begin to question all over again. I finally realized what I was experiencing was the "stupor of thought." Go figure. My indecisiveness and roller-coaster emotions were really an answer in and of themselves. As I set aside my emotions, searched the scriptures, and read the words of prophets and apostles, the answer to my dilemma was crystal clear. I then felt immense peace and all my uneasiness subsided. I was so thankful I didn't act on a whim.

When we learn to discern between our own emotions and the gentle whisperings of the Holy Spirit, we fine-tune our ability to receive promptings. It is through the power of discernment that we can ensure that our choices are indeed right. So, remember, our greatest protection, against the wiles of the adversary lies in seeking out the "highest source" and then listening for the still small voice to give us a confirmation. Elder Richard G. Scott said: "Carefully study the scriptures and counsel of the prophets to understand how the Lord wants you to live. Then evaluate each part of your life and make any adjustments needed. . . . When in doubt, ask yourself, "Is this what the Savior would want me to do?"[7] This is how we avoid being deceived.

THE VIRTUE TEST

Something that has helped me discern my emotions from the promptings of the spirit is something I call "The Virtue Test." It is this:

1. *Does what I desire measure up to the principles and standards of the Church?* What do the scriptures teach on this matter? What commandments, standards, and principles pertain? What counsel has been given by Latter-day prophets, apostles, general authorities, and other Church leaders?

2. *Does what I desire lead me closer to Christ or pull me*

further away? If Christ were standing next to me what would I choose? How does what I want fit into the bigger picture of my eternal salvation? Would Christ choose it?

3. *Is what I want pure and holy?* Does my choice glorify God? Does it affect the greater good of others? Is it pure? Is it holy?

4. *Am I pleasing God by what I am doing?* What would my Heavenly Father want me to do? Am I being true to the virtue of who I am as a daughter of God? Am I focusing on God and what He wants for me?

THE ADVERSARY'S FORMULA FOR DECEPTION

The strategies Satan uses to tempt women of today are as different and distinct as the women he tempts. The temptations are a customized fit! Satan knows Jane isn't tempted by yellow, but she is attracted to green so that's where he'll concentrate his efforts. And Joan isn't tempted by purple, so he'll use red and orange to distract her. See how that works? How do we protect ourselves against these customized attacks? By studying and applying the doctrine, principles, and standards of the Church. Elder Henry B. Eyring said the following during the first worldwide leadership training broadcast: "The Lord has given us His standards of worthiness. He has not done it to keep us away from Him but to draw us *to* Him."[8] The adversary would love for us to believe that the Church's standards are forms of restriction. He has even developed a tried-and-true formula of deception so he can gain power over us. Our brother Nephi warned us of this tactic in the Book of Mormon. What is this tactic Satan uses? Passivity. "And others will he *pacify*, and lull them away into carnal security, that they will say: All is well in Zion; yea, Zion prospereth, all is well and thus the devil cheateth their souls, and leadeth them away carefully down to hell" (2 Nephi 28:21, emphasis added).

Of course, Satan wants us to think all *is* well. He'd like us to sit on a comfy couch with our feet propped up and ordering room service from our cozy suite in his Big and Spacious Inn! That way, he'll have a better chance at "carefully" leading us away. (And he's not leading us on a nice long vacation in the Caribbean, mind you!)

THERE IS PROTECTION IN THE WORD OF GOD

Our best defense against the adversary is the virtue of the word, the word of God. The "*word* had a great tendency to lead the people to do that which was just . . . therefore Alma thought it was expedient that they should *try* the virtue of the word of God" (Alma 31:5, emphasis added). To protect ourselves from worldly temptations, we must *try* the virtue of the word. We must seek it out, study it, pray about it, and apply it to the decisions we make in our lives.

The scriptures teach that "the glory of God is intelligence" (D&C 93:36). Knowledge means *knowing*. But intelligence is the act of *applying* that knowledge. An intelligent woman will act on what she knows. So the glory comes not in just *having* the knowledge but in *applying* and *trying* it.

President Hinckley said in the September 2007 Ensign, "I plead with you my [sisters], that if you have any doubt concerning any doctrine of this Church, that you put it to the test. Try it. Live the principle. Get on your knees and pray about it, and God will bless you with a knowledge of the truth of this work."[9] In summary, the "word" is our protection. It is our armor. It is our shield.

Notes

1. Robert L. Millet, *I Will Fear No Evil* (Salt Lake City: Deseret Book, 2002), 127.

2. Kimball, "Always a Convert Church: Some Lessons to learn and Apply This year."

3. Millet, *I Will Fear No Evil*, 119.

4. Harold B. Lee as quoted in Campbell, "Challenges of the '80s."

5. Ibid.

6. Faust, "The Forces That Will Save Us."

7. Richard G. Scott, "Removing Barriers to Happiness," *Ensign,* May 1998, 85.

8. Henry B. Eyring, as quoted in Gibbons, "Wherefore, Settle This in Your Hearts." Emphasis added.

9. Gordon B. Hinckley, "Inspirational Thoughts," Ensign, Sep. 2007, 4.

7

The Little Matters of Virtue

WHATSOEVER THINGS ARE PURE, WHATSOEVER THINGS ARE LOVELY,
WHATSOEVER THINGS ARE OF GOOD REPORT; IF THERE BE ANY VIRTUE,
AND IF THERE BE ANY PRAISE, THINK ON THESE THINGS.
—Philippians 4:8

After speaking to a group of mothers and daughters, a woman approached me and said, "You know it's the little things you have to watch out for." And she was right in her thinking. Each and every day our character is being tested by "little" matters of virtue. Like what we're going to wear. What we're going to watch. How we're going to spend our time. These are the "little" things that in the big scheme of things *do* make a difference. Mother Teresa once said, "Be faithful in small things because it is in them that your strength lies." This same message is reflected in the scripture that says, "Out of small things proceedeth that which is great" (D&C 64:33).

President Hinckley recalled a story that relates to this idea of being faithful in "small things." He stated: "I recall a bishop telling me of a woman who came to get a [temple] recommend. When asked if she observed the Word of Wisdom, she said that she occasionally drank a cup of coffee. She said, "Now, bishop, you're not going to let that keep me from going to the temple, are you?" To which he replied, "Sister, surely you will not let a cup of coffee stand between you and the House of the Lord."[1]

There are those things in our lives that seem so small, so insignificant; yet, they can be big enough to distance us from the Lord, making them not so small after all. I like to call these small things "silly things." And you know who is good at easing us in to our silly things? The adversary.

Silly things are all around us, pressuring us to give in a little here and a little there. Silly things can be habits, hobbies, grudges, attitudes, behaviors, or interests. A silly thing could be something we wear. Something we do. Something we say. Something we desire. Something we can't seem to live without. Whatever our silly thing is, if it stands between us and the Lord; if it takes our focus off the things that really matter, it isn't such a "silly" thing, is it?

Several years ago, I was with a group of women who decided to do something "just for fun." It was something that went against my better judgment of what was right. Now, please understand these women were *good* women, whom the Lord loved and cherished just as much as he did me. But, I felt uneasy about what these women wanted to do. It was just enough on the edge of what I considered to be worldly so I said, "No. It's not for me." Was I prudish? I don't think so. I just preferred not to drift, wander, or dabble.[2] For me that was and always will be good advice. It felt right then, and it still feels right today. Deep down inside, I simply didn't want a "silly thing" to stand between me and the Lord. And so I chose to walk away.

"The Lord needs women who will take upon themselves his ways, his will, and his work, as well as his name."[3] We can't do that whole-heartedly if we're hanging onto our "silly things." Let us not be afraid to draw the line between right and wrong, good and evil. Let's let go of the silly things that, well, are just *silly*! If we do "the heavens will shake for [our] good" (D&C 21:6). Why would we want to settle for anything less? Why would we want to compromise our virtue with such silliness?

IT'S OKAY TO LET YOUR HAIR DOWN

Does not being "silly" mean we have to be so serious that we can't ever have fun and play? Of course not. It's good to laugh and enjoy! One night after Young Women's, I decided to have some fun. I and another leader were driving a few girls home after an activity. We had been Christmas caroling at the House of Hope where I volunteer. We had had a wonderful time, and the car was filled up to the brim with Christmas cheer. Before we dropped of the first girl, I had an idea. I knew a member of the bishopric and his family well. One of his daughters was in my class. Well, Brother Norton had a plastic Christmas nativity on display in his front yard. I thought it might be fun to play a "switch-a-roo" and place his nativity set in my brother's front yard, which was next door. I told the girls my brother had "nativity envy." (You see, Brother Norton's yard was all lit up with lights and my brother's was, well, let's just say "bare as bones.")

The girls were more than excited to do the "switch-a-roo." We started laughing before we even stopped the car. We parked about twenty feet away from the "site" and crept carefully over to the scene. Debbie, the "wise" leader, who decided to stay in the "lookout" vehicle, had rolled down her window so she could coach us a bit (actually, I think she just wanted us to hear her laughing hysterically, which she did when she saw what happened next). Elizabeth grabbed a shepherd and I grabbed one of the kings. But as we lifted them up off the ground and started to dart away, we realized they were attached to electrical cords. And those cords were attached to the "motherboard." Before we knew it we had short-circuited the entire Christmas light display. And within seconds, who should open the front door to the house but Brother Norton himself (and did I mention he was also a sheriff?).

There I was with my girls caught red-handed (or should I say king-handed?). The girls ran. And there I stood to face Brother Norton all alone with one of the three kings. All I could think of to say was, "So does this mean I'm getting an early release?" Debbie and the other girls were roaring! Just then who should drive up to the front of the house with her Suburban brights a blaring? It was Sister Norton with five other Young Women there to witness my debut. How embarrassing! Thankfully Brother Norton (and his wife) found this to be funny, too. He announced in sacrament meeting the next Sunday that the Young Women were graciously trying to do as Jesus would do by "sharing" nativities with those who were "less fortunate" than he and to be on the "look out." Yes, it's good to laugh. It's good to play. And, yes, there are those times when we in good, clean fun we can let our hair down (just a little).

WHEN STANDING UP FOR WHAT'S RIGHT, WE'RE IN GOOD COMPANY

Julie B. Beck, while serving as first counselor in the Young Women general presidency, said: "We have an obligation to speak up and lead out in what is right and true in the world around us."[4] None of us likes to go against the grain. None of us likes to stand out and be different. But when being different means we're on the Lord's side, that's a good thing. And when we're standing up for what's right we're always in good company.

We're in the company of Joseph Smith, Abinadi, Moroni, King Benjamin, Jacob, and Moses. And Noah! Just think about Noah for a minute. Think about what he was up against while he was building a giant boat (not to mention a giant boat sitting a top dry ground!). God told Noah to tell the people a flood was coming and so he did. And God told Noah to build a boat. And so he built one. Imagine what his neighbors must have thought as they saw him work on a boat day after day in the middle of a dry season.

"What have you got here, Noah?"

"I'm building a boat because a flood is coming," Noah replied. "And you'd do well to prepare, too."

"Oh, you silly man, Noah. It doesn't look like rain to us," the crowd taunted.

"No, it probably doesn't. But it *is* going to rain," Noah said.

"Oh, we'll you're just 'Noah the know-it-all,' aren't you? See you later, Noah. You just keep building and we'll just keep laughing."

Of Noah's steadfast strength, President Thomas S. Monson said in the October 2002 general conference: "Noah had the unwavering faith to follow God's commandments. May we ever do likewise. May we remember that the wisdom of God oftentimes appears as foolishness to men; but the greatest lesson we can learn in mortality is that when God speaks and we obey, we will always be right."[5]

When we're standing with God, his prophets, and his apostles we'll always be right, even when we're standing alone. Standing with God means standing in the right place, at the right time, for the right reasons. It may not always mean we're standing in a crowd, enjoying the camaraderie of the group, for there will be times when we find ourselves standing alone. In these moments, however, let us remember whose company we're in, for we are never really alone. "Rejoice, and be exceeding[ly] glad: for great is your reward in heaven: for so persecuted they the prophets which were before you" (Matthew 5:12). That scripture found its way to me through a lovely homemade card made by a dear and inspired Relief Society president. Those words reached out to me in a time of great need—a time when I had chosen to stand up and found myself standing alone. In times like these, we must keep the faith! Even though others aren't standing with us, there *will be* others who *will* gain strength from *our* strength. Others will find the courage to stand tall through us. And together we will stand even taller.

SILLY THINGS AND DISCRETIONARY TIME

Elder M. Russell Ballard of the quorum of the Twelve Apostles has stated: "One of the ways Satan lessens your effectiveness and weakens your spiritual strength is by encouraging you to spend large blocks of your time doing things that matter very little. . . . One devastating effect of idling away our time is that it deflects us from focusing on the things that matter most."[6] Spending time on things that, in the big scheme of things, matter very little weakens our spiritual strength. A powerful Relief Society lesson, shared with me through another sister, taught me the concept of the "weightier matters." This object lesson had such an impact on me that I have never forgotten it. The teacher asked the class to do the following: "For one week, read this commandment each morning, noon, and night: *Thou shalt have no other Gods before me.* Then ask yourself, 'Who is my God today? Right now? See how having this perspective changes the choices you make. Take notes throughout the week and come prepared to share what you discovered in Relief Society this coming Sunday."

Well, as you may have guessed, hearing about this challenge made me think about everything little thing I was doing. Because of this assignment, I chose to pray a little longer and more often. I chose to read my scriptures more often, even several times throughout each day. I chose to judge which activities to be involved in using greater clarity and discernment. I wanted to make sure everything I did showed God that He came first and that I was doing what I was doing because I loved the Lord.

If God were really our first priority, and everything we chose fit into that priority scheme, how much different would our lives be? This is definitely something to ponder. Try this exercise. See what results.

In all of our seeking, let us make room for the things that matter most. Let us seek after "whatsoever things are pure, whatsoever things are lovely, whatsoever things are of good report; if there be any virtue, and if there be any praise" let us seek after these things (Philippians 4:8; Articles of Faith 1:13). "Remember faith, virtue, knowledge, temperance, patience, brotherly kindness, godliness, charity, humility, diligence" (D&C 4:6). These are the "weightier matters" that should take precedence over any "little" matters. Let us be faithful in the little things so the Lord will bless us greater.

NOTES

1. Hinckley, "The Body Is Sacred."

2. Gibbons, "Wherefore, Settle This in Your Hearts."

3. Elaine A. Cannon, "Daughters of God," in *The Best of Women's Conference* (Salt Lake City: Bookcraft, 2000), 101.

4. Julie B. Beck, "Thou Art an Elect Lady Whom I Have Called," in *The Best of Women's Conference 2006* (Salt Lake City: Bookcraft, 2007), 30.

5. Thomas S. Monson, "Models to Live By," *Ensign,* Nov. 2002, 60.

6. Ballard, "Be Strong in the Lord."

8

The Beauty of Purity, Not Perfectionism

PRACTISE VIRTUE AND HOLINESS BEFORE ME CONTINUALLY.

—D&C 46:33

Let's turn now to Proverbs 31, the famous chapter on "The Virtuous Woman." Here we learn what the Lord expects a virtuous woman should do. A virtuous woman:

- should plead the cause of the poor and needy (v. 9)
- is priced far above rubies (v. 10)
- is safely trusted (v. 11)
- does good (v. 12)
- works willingly (v. 13)
- gives meat to her household including handmaids (in other words, she shares and consecrates her blessings with others) (v. 15)
- has skills; is talented; works with her hands—she plants, she uses the spindle, distaff, and makes linens. (This is proof that multitasking is a spiritual endeavor! Virtuous women are multitaskers! They are busy and involved and engaged in good works.) (vv. 16, 18, 24)
- she girdeth her loins with strength (v. 17)
- stretches out her hand to the poor and needy (v. 19)
- is not afraid of snow (which means she is prepared for hard

times, and she clothes and prepares her family) (v. 21)

- she brings honor to her husband (v. 23)
- has strength and honor as her clothing (meaning she is not concerned with worldly things) (v. 25)
- she seeks wisdom, is intelligent, speaks kindness (v. 26)
- is not idle (v. 27)
- her children and husband call her blessed and praise her (v. 28)
- she is exalted (v. 29)
- she knows beauty alone is vain and knows that a woman who fears the Lord shall be praised (v. 30)

Now, this listing of Proverbial attributes is not for the purpose of causing distress or discomfort. I say that because I know some of you are immediately using it as a measuring stick to note your deficiencies. And that isn't the purpose of these scriptures. It can be the nature of women to beat themselves up for what they are not doing instead of rewarding themselves for what they are doing well. Why must we be so hard ourselves? We shouldn't be. We need to be gentle with ourselves and recognize all the good we are doing because we are doing a lot. The Lord knows it, and he is willing to bless us because of it.

One of the challenges we face as modern-day women is perfectionism. And, sisters, in our quest to be virtuous we must remember this eternal truth. (I really believe it is one of the most important truths a woman can understand.) **Virtuous women seek purity NOT perfectionism.** There is a vast difference between the two. Perfectionism is the world's way. *Purity is the Lord's way.*

Let's look closely at these two ways of being. Perfectionism versus purity.

Perfectionism is defined as "a propensity for being displeased with anything that is not perfect or does not meet extremely high standards."[1] Having high standards—that's a good thing, right? Yes, having high standards can help us reach our goals; however, by definition perfectionism is a tendency to be *displeased* with anything that is not perfect. Being displeased doesn't fit the definition of perfection in the way the Lord defines it to be. Our Savior and Heavenly Father are not constantly "displeased" with us because we are not perfect. They are not constantly waving their finger at us saying, "Shame. Shame on you." No! They are our best cheerleaders always full of encouragement, hope, patience, and love. They are the cheerleaders in the sidelines telling us to stay focused on the positive and forgo the negative.

Sometimes we understand a concept better if we look at its opposite. So, let's look at the opposite of being displeased. What might that look like? I think it looks like being pleased, happy, positive, content, and optimistic. It looks like being grateful for we've been given; it looks like being humble as we accept our weaknesses; it looks like being pleasantly hopeful as we strive to be better in our journey towards perfection. President of BYU, Cecil O. Samuelson states:

> There is an understandable goal to follow the Savior's direction to "be ye therefore perfect" (Matthew 5:48). While this goal is admirable and appropriate, it is unfortunate that some consider that this perfection must occur immediately. A careful study of the footnote. . . to this verse teaches us that the notion of being perfect means that we are "complete, finished, [and] fully developed." Thus, while we should be engaged in the process of perfection, we need to acknowledge that achieving this goal will likely take a long time for all of us. The Lord said, "Ye are not able to abide the presence of God now, neither the ministering of angels; wherefore, continue in patience until ye are perfected" (D&C 67:13). This is good advice for all of us. There clearly are some things in which you can be perfect. The payment of tithing and the behavioral aspects of the law of chastity are examples. There are other things, however, that most of us will need to work on throughout our entire lives and yet not reach the perfection that is eventually promised until the eternities if we are true and faithful. Matters such as having absolute faith in the Lord Jesus Christ, a complete understanding of the scriptures, always controlling our thoughts and our tongues are all issues that require persistence and patience.[2]

Remember in striving to "be ye therefore perfect" that we are striving for a "pure" heart not a "perfect" heart. Becoming perfect is not a lifetime endeavor; it is an eternal endeavor. We read in Moroni: "Yea, come unto Christ, and be perfected in him, and deny yourselves of all ungodliness; and if ye shall deny yourselves of all ungodliness, and love God with all your might, mind and strength, *then* is his grace sufficient for you, that by his grace ye may be perfect in Christ; and if by the grace of God ye are perfect in Christ, ye can in nowise deny the power of God" (Moroni 10:32, emphasis added).

This scripture teaches us the requirements for purity: (1) coming unto Christ, (2) denying ourselves of ungodliness, and (3) loving God with our might, mind, and strength. "Therefore, marvel not at these things, for ye are not yet pure; ye can not yet bear my glory; but ye shall behold it *if* ye are faithful in keeping all my words that I have given you" (D&C 136:37, emphasis added). When I finally understood this concept that the Savior was asking me to become pure so that in Him I could become perfect it was life changing! Why? Because being perfect I knew I could never be; however, striving to be pure is something I could do. In God's omnipotent wisdom He provided us a way to become pure through the Atonement. "Ye that are pure in heart . . . *receive* the pleasing word of God" (Jacob 3:2, emphasis added). The "word" tells us to repent. And when we do, through the "virtue of [the Savior's] blood" (D&C 38:4) we are made pure. That seems so much more attainable than perfection.

Each of us at some time in some way has acted less then we ought to have. At times we have placed our treasures and our hearts on less than virtuous thoughts, desires, and actions. But from those lesser moments we can begin anew. We can begin to identify our own personal stumbling blocks, remove them from our path, and turn away from evil influences. We can plant our feet firmly on the path of virtue and do the work of virtuous women by losing ourselves in the service of God (Mosiah 2:17). We can once again discover beauty is found not in what we can do on our own but what we can do with God.

BECOMING PURE IS ABOUT FORGIVING OURSELVES

We've all fallen down, skinned our knee, and waited for the scrape to heal. Cared for properly, the wound eventually heals and the scar even fades. It is Satan who wants us to believe that unvirtuous living leaves scars that can never be healed. But that is not true. Through repentance our spirits can once again become pure. Through the power of Jesus Christ, our virtue can be restored.

It is virtuous to always exercise compassion toward ourselves and others because we are forever going to be learning, growing, and healing. Throughout our lives each of us *will* experience our own "Personal Tests of Virtue." This is part of Heavenly Father's plan of happiness. Heavenly Father set forth in the Garden of Eden this precedence: "We will prove them herewith, to see if they will do *all* things whatsoever the Lord their God shall command them" (Abraham 3:25, emphasis added). You can bet we will face opposition as we strive to live a more virtuous life. Joseph Smith stated: "The nearer a person approaches the Lord, a greater power will be made manifest by the adversary to prevent the accomplishment of His purposes."[3] It will be during these tests that we will find out where our strengths and weaknesses lie. As Christian writer C. S. Lewis said, "You find out the strength of the wind by trying to walk against it, not be lying down."[4]

BROKEN VIRTUE

Our Savior knows, somewhere along our path, we will experience the sadness that comes from broken virtue. Some will experience the consequences of their own broken virtue while others will experience the pain from another's. Shelley, I'll call her, gave me permission to share her story. She came to me one Sunday morning as I was finishing up the breakfast dishes.

I heard an abrupt knock at my door and looked at the clock. *10:00 AM on a Sabbath morning? Who could it be?* I wondered. It wasn't fast Sunday, so I knew it couldn't be the deacons coming to collect fast offerings. I opened the door to see a dear friend from across town standing on my porch, and I knew something must be wrong. With a quick "hello and come in" we made our way to my basement office, where I quickly shut the door. The words that followed were heart wrenching. Her marriage of eighteen years had been compromised, and she was suffering immeasurably. I could not bear to imagine my friend's heartache. Our friendship was deep. We were as close as two women who were not related could possibly be. After a long visit and discussion about what was going to happen, we hugged one another and said a prayer. Her departure left me feeling uneasy, knowing a tornado had just swooped through her life and the only thing she could do was head home to begin picking up the pieces.

Satan's cunning devices had threatened the sanctity of my friend's eternal family. I was hurting deeply for my friend. I knew she was willing to try to restore her family, but the road ahead would be difficult and much was still unknown. She was so weary and so very sad. She was (and still is) one of the best women I have ever known, and I knew she would live up to her temple covenants, listen to the spirit, and follow the Lord. "Through the Atonement I was able to forgive and move forward," Shelley said. "I held onto the Savior. And He held onto me." She told me: "Although, the road has been rocky, even at times seemingly unbearable,

I have experienced the peace that comes through the Savior's Atonement. I have seen the hand of the Lord in my life, over and over again. He has been my rock and my Redeemer. The Lord has solved problems for me that I never could have solved on my own. He has carried me and strengthened me and my children. I would go through it all again to know what I know now."

Go through it all again? Go through heartache, pain, and disappointment all over again? Yes, she would. Just to know the Savior as she now knows Him today. Shelly has been a great strength to me as I have watched her, in partnership with the Lord, rise up and strengthen her family as a woman of virtue steadfast in the Lord Jesus Christ.

Sisters, the Lord knows about deep wounds caused by broken virtue. In the Book of Mormon, when wickedness among the Nephites was rampant, and "abominations" were being practiced before the Lord, the prophet Jacob spoke plainly to his people and called them to repentance. Jacob apologized for his boldness in speaking: "It grieveth me that I must use so much boldness of speech concerning you, before . . . many of whose feelings are exceedingly tender and chaste and delicate before God, which thing is pleasing unto God" (Jacob 2:7). Oh, how the Lord values the tender, chaste, and delicate nature of women. And the prophet Jacob knew this. "For behold, I the Lord, have seen the sorrow, and heard the mourning of the daughters of my people" (Jacob 2:31).

Like these women, in Book of Mormon times, daughters, wives, mothers, and children sometimes mourn as they are subjected to harsh and unvirtuous realities. Broken virtue brings sadness and sorrow, but let us be comforted in knowing the Lord will not have us suffer alone. He hears our weeping, and he weeps with us. He hears our pleadings, and he pleads for us. He hears our prayers, and he answers them. When our burdens are too heavy and our sorrows run too deep, he carries us and makes our burdens light. The Savior's Atonement is an infinite Atonement and covers everything. Whether it is for the transgressor or the transgressed, the Atonement of Jesus Christ is the healing balm of Gilead. It will bind up our wounds, heal our hearts, and strengthen our spirits. We all need healing. Oh, how we need it!

FINE-TUNING AND POLISHING OUR CHARACTER ONE VIRTUE AT A TIME

When my daughter started playing the flute in the fifth grade, we bought her a used flute. It was twenty years old and hadn't been played in eighteen years. It was tarnished and sounded airy. An expert technician told us it needed some minor adjustments, but it had the potential to make beautiful music. I couldn't believe how different the flute sounded after its tune-up. The notes that once sounded hollow and airy were soon full and vibrant. The polishing also made the once tarnished silver shine like new! The flute looked beautiful and sounded beautiful, too.

Like this instrument, each of us can fine-tune our character and with the Lord's help, turn our weaknesses into strengths (Ether 12:27). President Hinckley told us to do the best we can with what we have and then do a little better than that. He stated: "I speak of the need for a little more effort, a little more self-discipline, a little more consecrated effort in the direction of excellence in our lives. . . . Let us all try to stand a little taller, rise a little higher, be a little better. Make the extra effort."[5] Are there a few small and simple virtues in your life that might need some fine-tuning and polishing?

The Lord Will Take Care When We Do Our Part

A couple of summers ago, my children and I went back East to vacation with my extended family. At the end of our trip, my family and my brother's family, piled into a large motor home to begin a three-hour drive to the airport. After about two hours, my brother glanced down at the gas gage and exclaimed, "We are out of gas!" The motor home then chugged and we knew we were in trouble. We pulled off to the nearest exit. While passing through the intersection all we could see were warehouses. No gas stations. Just buildings. It was a pretty rough area, certainly one we didn't want to be out walking around in—especially with children. At this point our older kids got scared. "What will we do if we can't find a gas station? Are we going to miss our flight?" After chugging along for about four blocks, we noticed a sign that read "GAS" off in the distance. "Please, Lord, just get us a little further," we all prayed. "We're almost there." Incredibly we made it all the way to the edge of the parking lot before the motor stopped and we began to coast. Would you believe the motor home came to a *complete* stop just ten feet away from the gas pump? We had made it! The pump, however, was still out of our reach. The hose wasn't long enough to reach the gas tank so we tried pushing the motor home closer but it was just too heavy. It wasn't going to budge. The Lord had taken us to a certain point but we would have to do the rest.

My brother bought a small gas can from the gas station attendant and used it to fill up the tank, one gallon at a time, until there was enough gas in the tank to flood the gas lines. After doing this about five times, the engine started and we were able to drive closer to the pump to finish filling up. Within thirty-five minutes we were back on the freeway and headed for the airport.

I learned from that experience that the Lord is willing to take care of us if we are willing to do our part. "And now, my daughter, fear not; I will do to thee all that thou requirest: for all the city of my people doth know that thou art a virtuous woman" (Ruth 3:11). This is an amazing promise! When we do *our* part to live virtuously, the Lord will fulfill his obligations to us. The key, however, is to remember that the Lord *does* require something of us first.

"And again, I say unto you, I give unto you a new commandment, that you may understand my will concerning you; Or, in other words, I give unto you directions how you may act before me, that it may turn to you for your salvation" (D&C 82:8–9).

The Lord has given us direction on how to be a virtuous woman. He has done so for our own good that we may someday attain salvation. He has also given us a *powerful* promise in Doctrine and Covenants 82:10: "I, the Lord, am *bound* when ye do what I say; but when ye do not what I say, ye have no promise" (D&C 82:10, emphasis added). *Bound* means compelled, duty-bound, inevitable, unavoidable, or obligated. The Lord is bound to bless us when we do what He says. The blessings may not be in the nice, neat package we're expecting. Nevertheless, if we do what he says, he is sure to bless us.

Does this mean the Lord takes away *all* of his support when we are not doing exactly what he asks of us? Not necessarily. He is a loving God and He may *choose* to bless us in spite of what we do or don't do.

To illustrate this point, I share this experience. I promised my children I would take them to get ice cream if they cleaned up their rooms and finished their homework. Right before we left, one of my children hit another sibling and got into trouble. I had to make a decision. Should I take this child who had done what I asked by cleaning up her room and finishing her homework? Or because she hit her little brother, should I choose to leave her at home? Now, technically she had fulfilled her responsibility. Her wrong choice pertained to something unrelated. I didn't feel *bound* to reward her with an ice cream cone. But I *chose* to let her come anyway and handled the hitting incidence by giving her another consequence. That was my choice. Just like this example, the Lord has to make choices similar to this all of time. (I wonder if it just wears Him out!) The key thing to remember is the Lord is only *bound* to do what we require when we are following Him and His ways.

ANGELS WILL BEAR YOU UP

Fighting the forces of evil can be daunting (even for Superwomen). So remember, when you're feeling overwhelmed, when the battlefield seems to be skewed to the devil's side, or when you're feeling afraid for yourself, your family members, a friend, or a loved one who is heading into unvirtuous territory, take comfort in this promise: "And whoso receiveth you, there I will be also, for I will go before your face. I will be on your right hand and on your left, and my Spirit shall be in your hearts, and mine angels round about you, to bear you up" (D&C 84:88).

You are not alone. Jesus Christ will fight with you to save souls whether it be your own, or one of your sisters or brothers. The scriptures assure us that the Lord will fight our battles (D&C 105:14). We can not do it alone. We dare not try. When you are struggling, when your energy reserves are low, when you feel less than who you ought to be; when you feel as if you are short of Heavenly Father's expectations; find solace in the words of Isaiah: "Hast thou not known? hast thou not heard, that the everlasting God, the Lord, the Creator of the ends of the earth, fainteth not, neither is weary? there is no searching of his understanding. He giveth power to the faint; and to them that have no might he increaseth strength. . . . They that wait upon the Lord shall renew their strength; they shall mount up with wings as eagles; they shall run, and not be weary; and they shall walk, and not faint" (Isaiah 40:28–31).

The Lord *will* renew your strength and he *will* empower you to do whatever the Lord requires. If we will seek after what is pure, great blessings of strength and support will come from on high (Philippians 4:8). "If [we] live up to [our] privileges, the angels cannot be restrained from being [our] associates."[6] Let us remember *always,* in our quest to become perfect we must first focus on becoming pure.

NOTES

1. Answers.com, "Perfectionism," http://www.answers.com/topic/perfectionism.
2. Cecil O. Samuelson, "What Does It Mean to Be Perfect?" *New Era*, Jan. 2006, 10.

3. Orson F. Whitney, *Life of Heber C. Kimball* (Bookcraft, 1967), 131, as quoted by Harold B. Lee, "May the Kingdom of God Go Forth," *Ensign,* Jan. 1973. 23.

4. C. S. Lewis, *Mere Christianity* (San Francisco: HarperCollins, 2001), 142.

5. Gordon B. Hinckley, "The Quest for Excellence," *Ensign*, Sep. 1999, 2.

6. Joseph Smith Jr., as quoted in "'She Shall Be Praised': Latter-day Prophets Speak to Women," *New Era*, Oct. 1974, 38.

9

The Greatest Virtue Is Charity

CLEAVE UNTO CHARITY, WHICH IS THE GREATEST OF ALL.
—Moroni 7:46

A few weeks after my first child was born, I flew back East to visit my parents. One night after I put my baby to sleep, I went looking for my mother and found her in the kitchen washing and drying the dishes. Seeing Mother standing there with the kitchen light bouncing off her shoulders, I found myself entranced by memories of all her simple acts of love—charitable acts. Like when I'd forget my lunch, and she'd drive clear across town (even on the busiest of days) to hand-deliver a brown, paper sack complete with sandwich, chips, dessert, drink, and, of course, one of her famous "napkin notes." The napkin greeting usually went something like this: "This is Meals on Wheels from your Mom! Have a great day. I love you!" Oh, how I loved those notes! (And my friends did too.) Now, in all honesty, I wasn't in elementary school. I wasn't even in junior high. I was in high school and missing a meal certainly wouldn't have killed me. But Mother simply would not have it. That's when I realized the purpose of my mother's service. It was much more than making sure I was well-fed. Her service was an act of charity. It was an act of love; an act of being there. I believe this is what charity is all about.

Growing up, my mother was always "there." Whether my mother was working in the family dry cleaners so we had extra money to take dance and singing lessons, sewing a skirt for my choir concert, or taking me and my friends to the mall, she did what needed doing. And, standing at the

85

sink doing the dishes that night, there she was again doing what needed to be done. And why? Because of love. Because of charity. To me, my mother is beautiful because of her simple acts of charity.

BUILDING UP OTHERS

The scriptures teach, "Cleave unto charity, which is the greatest of all [virtues]" (Moroni 7:46). Charity is the epitome of what a virtuous woman should strive to become. After all, when charity works inside a woman's heart, a desire grows to lift and build up others. When we are lifting and building up others, that is when we have true charity. I think of my sister in this way. When she was preparing to come to the United States for a visit, she wanted to bring her friend Tauta along. (I spoke of Tauta in an earlier chapter.) Where my sister lived in Albania, few people had ever been to the United States or would ever have the opportunity to do so. My sister wanted Tauta to experience America. To Tauta (her husband, family, and townspeople) this trip was an opportunity of a lifetime. On the day of the departure the plane left from the airport at 2 AM. Because it was so rare for someone in Tauta's city to visit America, many people went to the airport to see her off. They were even dressed in their Sunday best. That's how important this trip was to everyone.

I was so excited to meet Tauta. I had eagerly made plans to take her on sightseeing excursions to temple Square and up the canyon to see the beautiful fall leaves. All the while my sister was busy thinking and planning for the essentials—doctor and dentist visits. Her goal was to make sure Tauta went back to her country with a clean bill of health and—most important—new teeth. When Jen told our family members how Tauta was missing many of her molars, which made it impossible for her to chew certain foods, we too wanted to help. Jen asked family members to donate any money they would have spent on Christmas gifts for her and her family and help with the expenses of dental bills. Happily, we all pitched in. Thankfully, a dentist in my neighborhood graciously donated thousands of dollars of dental work and made it possible for Tauta to go home to her homeland with the most glorious set of teeth—the best set of teeth I have ever seen!

My sister knew the blessing of having good teeth and desired the same for her friend. Desiring something better for someone else—that is charity. My sister knows a new set of teeth won't change the world, but I can tell you they sure made one Albanian woman named Tauta smile a *giant* smile.

BE ANXIOUSLY ENGAGED IN GOOD WORKS

"Verily I say, [women] should be anxiously engaged in a good cause, and do many things of their own free will, and bring to pass much righteousness; For the power is in them, wherein they are agents unto themselves. And inasmuch as [women] do good they shall in nowise lose their reward" (D&C 58:27–29).

As sisters in the gospel of Jesus Christ, we are encouraged to be anxiously engaged in doing good. And so many do so much good! (I'm guessing the number of casseroles baked by Relief Society sisters is a Guinness Book world record! And if it isn't, it should be!) As sisters we reach out. We take care. We watch over. We encourage. We nurture. We support. This is who we are and what we're all about. We organize child care for sick neighbors. We run the PTA, Boy Scouts, Girl Scouts, neighborhood clean-up committees, election committees, and float-building committees. We care for the sick, the depressed, and the lonely. We bandage skinned knees, feed stray dogs, and carpool our kids plus the neighbors' kids (and sometimes kids we don't even know)! Much of the time we excel in service, and sometimes we *really* excel.

One dinner-making experience was most memorable. I, along with two other women in my neighborhood (let's call them Sister Red and Sister Blue) planned to surprise Sister Green with dinner. While I was busy assembling my manicotti noodles, Sister Red called to say she had come down with the flu and was sorry she couldn't help make dinner. So, I called Sister Blue, and the two of us decided to bring dinner to both Sister Green and Sister Red. Well, while making the salads and dessert, Sister Blue talked to Sister Yellow and found out that Sister Yellow had had a difficult week. So, Sister Blue called me back and suggested that we take dinner to Sister Green, Sister Red, *and* Sister Yellow.

"Sure. Why not?" I said, with ricotta cheese oozing from my pores. "The more manicotti the merrier!"

A little later on, we found out that another friend, Sister Purple, had had a family tragedy. We knew we couldn't leave her out, so we added Sister Purple to our recipient list. However, when we told Sister Yellow we were bringing her family dinner, she refused to accept it *unless* she could take a salad to Sister Green. Well, then Sister Purple found out the Sister Red had the flu and *she* insisted on sending her family ice cream sundaes! (After all, that was the least she could do if we were bringing her dinner!)

Isn't this just the epitome of what we do as sisters! Yes, it would have made more sense for all of us to make our own dinners and leave it at that. But what does that accomplish? We desire to have charity and we try hard to be there for one another in doing whatever needs doing.

CHARITY IS SEEING WITH DIFFERENT EYES

To have charity also means we see one another with different eyes. I think of a true story about a woman named Betty when I think of charity in this way. This story involves my father who was a director for the organization where Betty worked. This organization employed mentally- and physically-challenged individuals. Betty was one of the clients who, for fifteen years, had worked there crocheting hot pads. That was all she had ever known. Every day Betty rode a bus to work and while at work she would sit in a chair and crochet; day after day, and hour after hour, hot pad after hot pad.

"Betty just likes to crochet hot pads," the employees told my father. "You'll never get her to do anything else. That's all she knows. That's all she does." Well, my father thought differently. He saw Betty with different eyes. And so one day he asked Betty, "How would you like to do something besides crochet hot pads? How would you like to be a greeter and welcome our customers into our store?"

"Oh, no. Betty crochets hot pads," Betty responded. "Betty only crochets hot pads."

Well, my father asked Betty ever day of every week. And for weeks, she refused him.

"Betty, I know you can do this. Please think about it. We need you," my father encouraged. Finally, after much prodding and convincing, Betty decided to give greeting a try.

At first, she looked scared and uncomfortable. But all it took was one smiling customer to say: "Thank you!" Betty had suddenly caught on to the magic of greeting.

"Hello!" Betty would bubble with pure joy and excitement. "Welcome to our store! Come in!"

Betty's own sister couldn't believe Betty was doing something other than crocheting. "What did you do, John?" she asked my father. "How did you ever get her to leave her hot pads?" she wondered in amazement.

Well, Betty was a faithful greeter. She refused to leave her post until the exact second her shift ended. "I'm a greeter. My name's Betty," she'd say with pride. You know, in the big scheme of things, being a greeter might not seem all that significant; however, it was important to a certain woman named Betty. Betty is a child of God. God loves her. He wants her to be *all* that she can be. She needed someone to see her with different eyes. She needed someone to see her, to *really* see her, and recognize her potential. My father has affected the lives of many "Bettys" who just needed to be seen in different light. That is his special gift. (Thanks, Dad, for sharing your special gift with me.)

SERVICE TEACHES US TO LOOK WITH OUR HEARTS

This past summer I helped organize a neighborhood fund-raiser for an autistic school. My twelve-year-old daughter decided her contribution would be making a Bundt cake for the silent auction. When she pulled it out of the oven I reminded her, "Don't try to dump the cake out until it's cooled for thirty minutes. Otherwise, it will fall apart." Well, she didn't listen and came running to get me with a frustrated look on her face.

"It's ruined! It's cracked in three places. I'll just throw it out," she muttered.

"No. We can fix it. We'll make it work." I had never patched a cake before but gave it a whirl. I couldn't bring it back all the way but my efforts did improve it a bit.

"Someone will love your cake just the way it is!" I said hugging her and kissing her forehead.

I must admit I told my dad that he needed to bid on Jacqueline's cake. I didn't want her to be disappointed. She had such good intentions.

The time came for the auctioneer to read off the names of the silent auction winners. And the winner of the Bundt cake is . . . "Begonia!" I was surprised. My father didn't win the cake. I ran over to Begonia and said, "Thank you. Jacqueline was so worried no one would buy her cake because it broke when she took it out of the pan."

Begonia replied with a grin, "I don't eat with my eyes; I eat with my heart."

The scriptures teach that the world looks on the outward appearance but the Lord looks on the heart (1 Samuel 16:7). Charitable service helps us do that. For eight years, I have had the wonderful privilege of serving at a drug treatment center in downtown Salt Lake City called the House of Hope—an organization that helps women overcome drug and alcohol addiction. I have learned to see these women with different eyes. I have learned to see inside their hearts and their souls as I have tried to understand their struggles and adversities. I have laughed with these women. I have cried with them. I've prayed for them and when tough things have happened in my own life, they have prayed for me. Sharing my time and talents with these women has brought more compassion into my life for anyone affected by the tragedy of addiction. Thousands of women have stepped through the doors of the treatment center seeking hope and healing and I have loved all of them! (They are truly my addiction.) Serving these women has changed me. It has taught me no matter what our background, our culture, our heritage, as women, we are more alike than we are different.

When I began teaching classes at the treatment center years ago, I knew nothing about addiction or about the individuals who suffered from addiction. But today, my heart is full of love, compassion, and understanding for those who walk this path.

This past summer, as I was preparing to teach a class, I heard a voice behind me say, "Hi, Jodi. Remember me?" I looked back and saw a woman holding a baby. I didn't remember her name, but I recognized her face. She had been in the treatment program a few years earlier. Looking at my youngest daughter, who was about to turn two, the woman asked, "Oh, is this the baby you were pregnant with last time I was here?" Then she went on to say: "I want you to know that I scrapbook and tie fleece blankets because of you. I remember all you taught me. Remember when you taught us to tie fleece blankets?" And I did. As sad as I was to think that this woman was returning to treatment, which meant she had returned to her addiction, I was so glad to know that she was getting help. And I was especially glad that she had remembered me and what I had taught her. In a small way I knew I had made a difference. I was so thankful that she thought so too.

Yes, I teach these women skills. But they teach me so much more than I teach them. From them I learn how to have hope when the future is unknown; from them I learn how to forgive when forgiveness doesn't seem possible; from them I learn how failures turn into triumphs; and from them I learn that being beautiful is about rediscovering who you are. I have seen many of these women go on to great things: graduate from college, raise families, and become successful women in the community. These women are my teachers. They are my heroines!

TEACHING OUR CHILDREN TO HAVE CHARITY

Once my eldest daughter was asked, "What does your mom like to do in her spare time?" She responded, "Oh, she likes to help women." That was one of the biggest compliments I could have ever been given. (Thanks, Sue, for sharing that with me. Otherwise, I would have never known that's how my daughter saw me.) By giving away a little of ourselves to others and by learning to see others with different eyes, we learn the meaning of the Lord's commandment to love one another as He loves us. President Thomas S. Monson reminds us to open our hearts and to reach down and lift up those who are oppressed. He asks us give of our time, our talents, and our pocketbooks and show greater love for our fellowmen. President Hinckley reminded us, "The Lord has blessed us so abundantly. And the needs are so great. He has said, 'Inasmuch as ye have done it unto one of the least of these my brethren, ye have done it unto me' (Matthew 25:40)."[1] This scripture is a call to action to "do" what the Savior would do.

Doing what the Savior would do reminds me of a twelve-year-old girl, who voluntarily takes two dollars from her allowance each week to buy a box of cereal, which she then donates to the local food bank. If this young woman is exercising the principle of charity and practicing it at such an early age, I can't wait to see what she does in her future! I think of my young son who sees unfinished wooden cars at Walmart and asks if he can paint some for the kids who don't have any toys. If we don't teach our children charity, how will they know what charity is—what it looks like and what it feels like? It's important to let them experience it for themselves.

Joseph B. Wirthlin told us to be careful not to just *say* we love the Lord, but *show* him we love Him by giving charity. "True devotion means more than mouthing syllables. 'If ye love me, keep my commandments' (John 14:15), the Savior taught His disciples, and so He urges us today."[2] If we love the Lord we will serve one another. Let us give of our time and talents. When we do, we'll feel beautiful. I guarantee it! I never feel more beautiful than when I'm driving away from the treatment center, after teaching a class, reminiscing about the conversations I had with the wonderful women I served. In the words of song writer, Cherie Call, "it's what you give that makes you beautiful."[3]

It's not driving a fancy car or wearing designer jeans that make us feel beautiful. It's the excitement that comes from giving! The opportunities to give are endless! Community organizations, nursing homes, senior centers, schools, libraries, homeless shelters, children's programs, causes that support world hunger, poverty, and disease. A quick search on the Internet and you'll find a plethora of worthy causes to give to. Decide where your passion lies and then follow your passion. Let the Lord lead you to those he desires you to love and then love them! Love them. There are people who are lonely, hopeless, and sad. There are many who simply underestimate their worth. Lift them up! Find a way to make a difference! Get involved.

I know of a woman who, despite her busy schedule, delivers meals to shut-ins. I know of a mother who teaches physical education and music classes at a school for autistic children. Does she have a degree in either? Absolutely not. She just knows there is a need. I know of a young woman who collects teddy bears for a low-income children's program; a college student who started a non-profit business to raise money for mosquito tents to help eradicate malaria in Africa. There's nothing extraordinary about these individuals. They are just doing what needs doing. We can serve our communities and our world in so many ways! Ask the question, "What can I do to help?" and then get out there and go to work. Remember, all the Lord needs is willing hearts and helping hands. He's counting on us to be His hands.

I heard the most inspiring comment at Education Week in 2007. A man, on a very tight budget, decided he needed to find some way to give more to charity. So, every day at lunch he would order a 6" sub sandwich instead of a 12" sub sandwich. The difference in price between the two sandwiches was the amount he saved and gave to charity. A few dollars turned into tens of dollars and then hundreds of dollars. Wow! What a great idea! This small sacrifice to me was the equivalent of the Widow's Mite. Would you be willing to do the same? Would you be willing to give up half of a sub sandwich to lift the burden of another?

Look around you. What needs can *you* meet? What relief can *you* offer? What can *you* do to give? Carefully survey your life and make some decisions to change what you are doing so *you* can give more to those who are less fortunate than you. What a glorious feeling it would be to know that an individual received a college education because of your donations to the Church's Perpetual Education Fund. What a joyful feeling you would have knowing a hungry child ate three meals a day because of your sacrifice. What a glorious feeling it would be to know that a child has a backpack, books to read, and shoes to wear because you chose to give.

I believe the best cure for sadness, despondency, low self-esteem, anxiety, and hopelessness is found in giving selfless service! Decide today to walk in paths of service, to walk in paths of *giving*! According to your own special gifts, talents, and abilities, I know you will find hundreds of ways to *serve* and *give*! Each of us is uniquely qualified to serve in God's kingdom. Each of us has a different path to walk. Each of us has different capabilities, different talents, different ways in which we can reach out. Thank goodness we're not all carbon copies of one another! Different needs are met by different women. Keep in mind, in our differences lie our greatest strengths. Each of us, in our own way, can be somebody's angel by providing relief, comfort, and care. Doing so, in the name of Jesus Christ, will bring into our lives the blessings of love pouring down from heaven. I bear my personal witness that in serving and giving we lose ourselves, and then we find ourselves better human beings than we ever imagined possible.

An Angel of Charity

Several years ago, after attending a marriage ceremony for one of my cousins, I was walking my eighty-year-old Grandmother to her car. She was holding tightly onto my arm. As we were passing through the temple gates, there on the curb, sat a gentleman in a wheelchair, a beggar with a sign that read, "Will work for food." As I began rummaging through my purse for some change, my eighty-year-old grandmother quickly let go of my arm and high-tailed it over this man.

"Grandma, where are you going!" I chased after her as she fumbled through her purse.

I caught up with her just as she reached out to put several dollar bills in the man's hands. I steadied her and then pulled on her arm, hinting to her that we should get going. My grandmother wouldn't budge. She didn't just hand off her money to the man and turn to leave. No, that wouldn't do. Instead, she took this stranger's hands in hers, clasped her hands tightly around his, and talked to him. She asked him about his day. With a smile on her face, she wished him well. Minutes passed. I could feel the tears welling up in my eyes. In that act of compassion, I could literally see the hands of the Savior reaching down and giving comfort to this lonely soul. Grandmother was showing "one of the least of these" that the Lord loved him. Through her kind act of charity, this beggar was blessed to feel the love of the Lord (Matthew 25:40). On that day, my grandmother was that man's angel of charity. In that tender moment, it wasn't money that my grandmother gave away. She had given her love away—her love of the Savior.

REALLY LIVE!

In our quest to develop charity, we must learn to *really* live . . . by losing ourselves in the service of others and the service of our God. One of my all-time favorite quotes is from the late Marjorie Pay Hinckley, wife of President Gordon B. Hinckley. She stated:

> I don't want to drive up to the pearly gates in a shiny sports car, wearing beautifully, tailored clothes, my hair expertly coiffed, and with long, perfectly manicured fingernails. I want to drive up in a station wagon that has mud on the wheels from taking kids to scout camp. I want to be there with grass stains on my shoes from mowing Sister Schenk's lawn. I want to be there with a smudge of peanut butter on my shirt from making sandwiches for a sick neighbor's children. I want to be there with a little dirt under my fingernails from helping to weed someone's garden. I want to be there with children's sticky kisses on my cheeks and the tears of a friend on my shoulder. I want the Lord to know I was really here and that I really lived.[4]

Marjorie Pay Hinckley was beautiful because of charity.

CREATION'S MASTERPIECE

Sisters, in all of our getting, who are we becoming? Are we becoming great women of charity? We will be known at the heavenly gates as virtuous women by the virtues of what we have become. James E. Faust said we become great women by cultivating and employing "noble, womanly instincts of care and mercy, first to [our] family and then to others." He encouraged us to go about our "angelic cause of doing good" so that we not only become great women of today but ultimately queens in the eternities.[5]

In the words of President David O. McKay, "A beautiful, modest, gracious woman is creation's masterpiece. When to these virtues a woman possesses as guiding stars in her life righteousness and godliness and an irresistible impulse and desire to make others happy, no one will question if she be classed among those who are truly great."[6] President Hinckley said those who reach out to lift and serve others "will come to know a happiness . . . never known before."[7] Let us follow the wise counsel of the prophets and strive to become great women who are happy and beautiful because of charity.

Notes

1. Gordon B. Hinckley, "Reaching Down to Lift Another," *Liahona*, Jan. 2002, 60.

2. Joseph B. Wirthlin, "Two Guiding Lights," *Ensign*, Aug. 2007, 64.

3. Cherie Call, *He Gives Flowers to Everyone,* "Beautiful," 2002.

4. GoodReads, "Quotes by Marjorie Pay Hinckley," http://www.goodreads.com/author/quotes/226482.Marjorie_Pay_Hinckley.

5. James E. Faust, "How Near to the Angels," *Ensign*, May 1998, 95.

6. David O. McKay, as quoted in "She Shall Be Praised: Latter-day Day Prophets Speak to Women."

7. Gordon B. Hinckley, as quoted in Joseph B. Wirthlin, "The Abundant Life," *Liahona*, May 2006, 99.

10

A Modest Woman Is Beautiful

WOMEN ADORN THEMSELVES IN MODEST APPAREL . . .
PROFESSING GODLINESS WITH [THEIR] GOOD WORKS.
—1 TIMOTHY 2:9–10

Getting dressed. We do it every day. But how important is what we wear? It's just clothing, right? Or is it something more?

A few years ago my husband kindly informed me my dresses, pants, and shirts were invading *his* side of the closet. He then hinted at me to "do something about it . . . *or else*." That's all it took before my closet makeover was underway! I couldn't believe what I found in there; like the dress I wore to my wedding dinner fifteen years earlier. Could I fit into it four children later? No! Why was it still in my closet? I have no idea. What was really funny was when I picked up a maternity dress I wore while expecting my third child and I suddenly became nauseous—no kidding. Those red and white checks spun me into nightmares of endless cravings for Lucky Charms cereal, tortilla soup, and soda crackers. I immediately knew that dress had to go! (To the woman who bought it at the second-hand store, I'm so sorry if it has had the same affect on you.)

Hours later, sitting on my bed were six bulging, white, plastic garbage bags filled with all my "undesirables." People could learn a lot about me by looking at what was inside of those bags. They'd discover I liked chocolate and pasta with red sauce (the stains on my T-shirts were dead giveaways). They'd figure out that at one time I loved the color purple (thus the plethora of purple T-shirts). They'd also figure that I had a fetish for anything nautical (thus the navy suit jackets with gold buttons and football-sized shoulder-pads.)

Well, since that official "closet makeover," I've thought a lot about how clothing says something about the person who wears it. And, because of that, my closet has undergone several makeovers for a different reason; the reason is I have discovered getting dressed is something . . . well . . . it's about something *more than just clothing*.

MORE THAN CLOTHING

Modesty was instituted by God in the Garden of Eden with our first parents, Adam and Eve: "Unto Adam also and to his wife did the Lord God make coats of skins, and clothed them" (Genesis 3:21). "The Lord knew that the Fall had opened Adam's and Eve's eyes to their nakedness, as well as unleashing powerful new appetites and desires. Out of love for his children, he dressed them in coats of skins."[1] Isn't that beautiful? Because God loved Adam and Eve, He dressed them and desired to protect them! God wanted to help Adam and Eve protect their bodies, which He had created from both physical and spiritual elements. It is within this doctrine we learn that dressing ourselves is *more* than the clothing we wear.

Dressing modestly has two components. The first and basic principle of modesty is to cover our nakedness. The second principle of modesty is: "to communicate who we truly are as children of God and, by covenant, disciples of Christ."[2]

MODESTY AND IMMODESTY DEFINED

"The word *modesty* ultimately stems from the Latin term *modus,* meaning 'measure.' Hence modesty connotes balance. . . [and] moderation."[3] *Immodesty* is defined as anything that draws undue attention to you or your body.[4] Immodesty isn't merely exposed flesh. According to *For the Strength of Youth,* immodesty relates to excess, extremity, lack of restraint, outlandishness, intemperateness, and immoderation. Immodesty also includes: short shorts and skirts, tight clothing, shirts that do not cover the stomach, and other revealing attire. It also counsels us to wear clothing that covers the shoulder and to avoid clothing that is low-cut in the front or back. Being modest should be more than just following these simple do's and don'ts. Our desire to be modest should spring forth from a deep desire to keep sacred things sacred.

MODESTY SAFEGUARDS THE SACRED

Our bodies should be kept sacred like a temple. It was Jesus Himself who first compared His body to a temple (John 2:21). "Know ye not that ye are the temple of God, and that the Spirit of God dwelleth in you? If any man defile the temple of God, him shall God destroy; for the temple of God is holy, which temple ye are" (1 Corinthians 3:16–17).

When I think of making and keeping something sacred, I think of the "Parable of the Silverware," a story told by Elder F. Burton Howard in General Conference. Elder Howard and his wife were poor college students when they got engaged to be married. They registered their "wish" list for household items at a local department store. Looking at the list, Elder Howard was surprised to see that his fiancé had only one desire—to have a set of silverware.

Upon returning from their honeymoon, the newlyweds were a little shocked upon opening their gifts because they had not received a single silver knife or fork. Elder Howard said they joked about it and then "went on with [their] lives." Finally, after many years, the Howard's had acquired enough pieces of silver to use for dinner gatherings. But although Sister Howard was happy about having the silver, she never used it for common, ordinary occasions. She safeguarded what was important to her. Brother Howard writes:

> I noticed that the silverware never went to the many ward dinners she cooked, or never accompanied the many meals she made and sent to others who were sick or needy. It never went on picnics and never went camping. . . . The time came when we were called to go on a mission. I arrived home one day and was told that I had to rent a safe-deposit box for the silver. She didn't want to take it with us. She didn't want to leave it behind. And she didn't want to lose it. For years I thought she was just a bit eccentric, and then one day I realized that she had known for a long time something that I was just beginning to understand. *If you want something to last forever, you treat it differently.* You shield it and protect it. You never abuse it. You don't expose it to the elements. You don't make it common or ordinary. If it ever becomes tarnished, you lovingly polish it until it gleams like new. It becomes special because you have made it so, and it grows more beautiful and precious as time goes by.[5]

This is how we must see and care for our bodies. We must treat them differently than the world teaches us to treat them. We must dress our bodies in such a way that we protect them. We must shield our bodies and never abuse them. We must not expose them to the temporal elements nor make them common or ordinary in any way by flaunting them. And if ever we mistreat our bodies, we must, through prayer, seek repentance and forgiveness.

If we casually set aside our virtue from time to time by choosing to have different standards of dress just because we're on vacation, in our backyard, at the pool or the gym, just hanging out, or even because we consider the occasion to be "special" or "different," if we slack in our dress standards to accommodate the "whatevers," we will eventually tarnish our attitude toward sacred things. We will eventually lose our sense of sacredness for our bodies.

A TEST TO STAND UP AGAINST THE WORLD

Bruce R. McConkie taught plainly that "modesty in dress and grooming is related to salvation." He stated: "Conforming to dress and grooming standards is one of the tests the Lord imposes upon us to see if we will take counsel and to see if we can stand up against the pressures of the world."[6] Looking at modesty as a test to see if we'll follow the Lord certainly takes getting dressed to a whole new level.

So, how important is dressing modestly? It's important enough for our Church leaders to address it fifty-two times since 1971 in general conference, Church broadcasts, and Church magazines. Although the word *modest* is only mentioned once in the Bible, I find what it says about modesty to be quite profound. In 1 Timothy 2:9–10, we read: "Women adorn themselves in *modest* apparel . . . which becometh women professing godliness with good works" (emphasis added). Elder Robert C. Oaks states: "Now is the time to provide the world with an example of decency and modesty, an example of virtue and cleanliness."[7]

Sheri Dew wrote: "Women are ideally suited to model and teach modesty. . . . But they are also ideally positioned to . . . make modesty a virtue from a bygone era."[8] More or less, women have power to champion virtue but they also have power to demean it. Concerned with the immodesty in his time, President Spencer W. Kimball stated: "A spirit of immodesty has developed [and] nothing seems to be sacred. . . . I am sure that the immodest clothes that are worn by some of our young women, and their mothers, contribute directly and indirectly to the immorality of this age. Even fathers sometimes encourage it. . . . I am positive that the clothes we wear can be a tremendous factor in the gradual breakdown of our love of virtue, our steadfastness in chastity."[9] It is important to take this counsel seriously. Immodesty contributes to the breakdown of virtue. It is one of Satan's biggest power tools because it leads to lesser things.

DRESSING MODESTLY FOR ALL OCCASIONS

Not long ago, I was visiting a ward and a young woman got up to give a talk. Her presentation was excellent but her clothing was distracting. Her appearance did not fit her message. A man I knew well, who was also in that same Church meeting, made the comment to me, "I felt so uncomfortable for that young girl. Her clothing was so inappropriate I just had to look at the floor." I stopped to think. Here was a wonderful man, a worthy priesthood holder attending church in a chapel of worship, and he had to look at the floor because a young woman chose to be immodest. Oh, my dear sisters, what are we thinking? Or is it that we're *not* thinking?

Our number one goal in choosing to dress modestly is to have our confidence *and* the confidence of others "wax strong in the presence of God" (D&C 121:45). To achieve this we must follow these principles: (1) dress ourselves on the outside to mesh perfectly with who we are on the inside, and (2) choose our clothing as a backdrop to what we are saying and doing. In other words, our clothing shouldn't be the main focus.

We should dress like we're representatives of the Lord Jesus Christ. So, what would a representative of Christ wear? Imagine if we wore shirts that said: I stand for truth and righteousness. I belong to the Church of Jesus Christ of Latter-day Saints. I believe in chastity. I am good friend and neighbor. I value virtue. I love and honor my parents. I live within my means. I obey the prophets. I love God. (Really we don't even need to wear any words on our T-shirts if we're dressing modestly because we are already making a statement about who we are and what we believe.) It's important to remember that even without words, our clothing coveys messages about who we are, what we deem important, and whom we wish to please when we wear it.

PRINCIPLES OF MODESTY

I have created Seven Principles of Modesty to help us as we strive to develop a testimony of modesty:

1. A virtuous woman dresses modestly because she loves the Lord.
By dressing modestly, a daughter of God shows the Lord she is committed

to living the gospel in its fulness. She shows she is committed to following the Lord's ways, always. Just like uniforms, clothing signifies where our loyalty lies. We can't *almost* be on the Lord's side. We either are, or we aren't. We are either modest or we're not. Dressing modestly shows a commitment to following the Lord's commandments.

2. A virtuous woman keeps her eye single to the glory of God by choosing modest apparel in style, purpose, and price (D&C 4:5). *Single* means sole or only. To remain "singly" or solely focused on the things of God keeps us focused on what's most important. Being modest keeps us temperate in our desires. It keeps us focused on the things of eternity and not on the vain things of the world.

The higher law taught by the principle of modesty is unity—unity with God and unity with our fellowman. When we are modest, singly focused on God, we are "others-oriented" not "self-oriented." Ninety years before the coming of Christ, the Nephites gave of their substance to the poor and the needy and the sick. "And they did not wear costly apparel, yet they were neat and comely" (Alma 1:27). And the Lord prospered them. But only in a few short years, "the people of the church began to wax proud, because of their exceeding riches, and their fine silks, and their fine-twilled linen, and because of their many flocks and herds, and their gold and their silver, and all manner of precious things, which they had obtained by their industry; and in all these things were they lifted up in pride of their eyes, for they began to wear very costly apparel" (Alma 4:6). The Nephites began to turn their backs on the needy. They were not "others-oriented." They were "self-oriented." Because clothing can become a separating factor among people, the Apostle Paul taught that "women [should] adorn themselves in modest apparel, with shamefacedness and sobriety; not with broided hair, or gold, or pearls, or costly array" (1 Timothy 2:9). This scripture teaches the principle of moderation—our clothing choices should be moderate in style, purpose, and price.

3. A virtuous woman dresses modestly to be her own kind of beautiful. Modest clothing doesn't have to mean boring and plain. (And thank goodness for that! I'm known among my peers for liking a little "bling" now and again.) Modesty also does *not* infer that we can't be an individual with our own style and flair. In an article entitled, "Fads and Faith," the author quotes Brigham Young in saying: "If I were a lady and had a piece of cloth to make me a dress, I would cut it so as to cover my person handsomely and neatly; and whether it was cut according to the fashion or not, custom would soon make it beautiful."[10] Sisters, we need to think of modesty as having a style all our own. We'll always be our own kind beautiful, if we seek to dress the part of a modest and gracious daughter of God.

4. A virtuous woman desires to put her "best dress forward," being clean in style and in conduct. It's important to put our best dress forward by seeking to represent the Lord in the best way we possible can. "Be ye clean, that bear the vessels of the Lord" (Isaiah 52:11). Modest women are clean in dress and in conduct. Their clean style of dress reflects an exactness in keeping themselves spotless from worldliness (D&C 59:9). There are not too many things we can be "perfect" in but we can be "perfect" in modesty. Modest women avoid trendy styles that include raggedy, worn, and tattered clothing.[11] They don't wish to present an image that sends a message of being unclean and uncaring. It doesn't cost anything to be clean and well-groomed. It just requires a conscientious effort. And as far as our conduct goes, clean speech is always free.

5. A virtuous woman dresses with humility. Contrary to worldly opinions, clothing is not for the purpose of gaining the attention of onlookers. It is for covering and protecting the sacred body gifted to us by God. In the Church's online Guide to the Scriptures, the subject of modesty is accompanied by the words "Humble, Humility." In that same guide, modesty is defined as a "behavior or appearance that is humble, moderate, and decent. A modest person avoids excesses and pretensions."[12] By being modest we are showing humility to God while at the same time being fashionably faithful.

6. A virtuous woman is an example of decency for all occasions. Dressing to fit the occasion is an important part of modesty. Fitting the occasion means we "respect the occasion." Attending church services is a sacred event for the purpose of worshipping God, so dressing up is appropriate. Leaders have told us flip-flops are not appropriate for Sunday worship. Flip-flops may be easy, affordable, and comfortable, but as one Young Women's president described it, "They aren't reverent." Wearing flip-flops, and other casual-like shoes, doesn't show respect for the occasion of worship in a sacred place. That is what Church is—it is sacred. The chapel particularly is a sacred place. What we wear should show respect and should be "reverent." Church is about worshiping God. And girls, with all the sensitivity I can think of, I feel that we should address this idea that prom dresses are for the prom and *not* proper attire for Sunday worship. Last I checked, there is no disco ball hanging in the chapel. Would it be okay to leave the flounce and taffeta at home? You may look beautiful in your evening gowns but these dresses are meant for dining and dancing not the chapel. Church, especially sacrament meeting, is not about who went to homecoming and prom. It's about the Atonement of Jesus Christ. It's about renewing covenants. Remember, one of our goals in being modest is to not have our clothing be the main focus. Believe me, prom dresses worn in Sacrament meeting do become the main focus. And that's just not reverent.

Elder L. Todd Christopherson said: "We dress formally at church and other sacred occasions *not* because *we* are important, but because the *occasion* is important."[13] Remember, what is decent and appropriate for some occasions is not appropriate for others. Let's honor and respect the purpose of the occasion by choosing appropriate dress.

7. A virtuous woman respects, protects, and honors the virtue of others (especially, the holders of the holy priesthood of God). I believe this next principle, if understood correctly, could transform the way young women and women view the importance of dressing modestly. The apostle Paul taught the Saints how they should treat one another saying, "Be kindly affectioned one to another with brotherly love; in honour preferring one another" (Romans 12:10). There is no better way to show kindly affection, brotherly love, and honor toward our brothers in the gospel of Jesus Christ than to dress modestly. Young men and men who hold the holy priesthood of God are sons of God just as we are daughters of God. They should be able to count on *us* (we, the women and young women of the Church) to be influences of goodness and virtue. We expect the men to honor our virtue, we should honor theirs. How do we do that? By dressing modestly. We must hold ourselves to a higher standard than the women of the world. Absolutely, we should. When we dress modestly, we show kindness, brotherly love, and honor to our brethren. For the Lord said, "But I say unto you, That whosoever looketh on a woman to lust after her hath committed adultery with her already in his heart" (Matthew 5:28). The daughters of Eve and the sons of Adam should hold one another's virtue in the highest regard and, therefore, virtuous women must choose to stay within the bounds the Lord has set and his boundaries do include modesty.

A modest woman values virtue in herself and in others. She knows she plays a part in whether someone's thoughts are virtuous or unvirtuous.

She takes that quietly to heart and respectfully makes clothing choices that will lead her and those in her presence to have positive and virtuous experience.[14]

THE RESPONSIBILITY OF INVITING VIRTUE

Once I was visiting with a group of women discussing the topic of modesty and one participant made this comment: "Hey, don't put all of this pressure on the girls. Tell it to the guys!" Well, shortly after that encounter, a member of a bishopric quoted Elder Dallin H. Oaks who said in general conference: "Do not use your purchasing power to support moral degradation. . . . please understand that if you dress immodestly, you are magnifying this problem by becoming pornography to some of the men who see you."[15] Yes, each individual has the responsibility to control his/her own mind and to "garnish" his/her thoughts "unceasingly" (D&C 121:45). But that is a lot easier to do when women are dressed modestly. Let us choose *never* to diminish someone's virtue by dressing immodestly. Let us invite virtue into every encounter.

Sisters, in the age of fleshy fashions and shape-hugging styles, let us make our stand! Let us use our purchasing power to dress modestly because we have a deep love for God. Because we desire to safeguard the gift of having a body. Let us show a sacred admiration for the holders of the Priesthood and invite virtue to accompany us whenever we are in their presence. Let us profess godliness by wearing modest apparel; for the "fashions of the world passeth away" but the beauty of a virtuous woman is forever.[16]

TOO AT EASE WITH THE TIGHT

I have to admit spandex *is* one the marvelous inventions of the twenty-first century. I am thankful for the ease and comfort that stretchy material provides my wardrobe. Too bad our pioneer sisters never had the luxury of stretchy pinafores. However, there is a downside to stretchy fabric; it allows us to "shrink" into our clothing at the expense of being modest. This is where we need to be careful to not become "too at ease with the tight." Founder and President of Conselle Institute of Image Management, Judith Rasband, said research shows that tight clothing communicates the message, "Look at me . . . I'm open to advances."[17] Ms. Rasband states:

> Many people think immodest dress relates only to an insufficiently

covered body. But a tight fit is also immodest, even when the body is fully covered. . . . Tight clothing draws attention to the anatomy [which can be just as revealing as wearing little or bare clothing], distracts from the purpose of education, business, leadership, or worship. Adequate ease in the fit of our clothes allows the viewer's attention to go to the other person's face for more effective communication.[18]

There are ways to wear stretchy fabrics modestly. Layering T-shirts are wonderful for what they were made for—layering. You can wear a stretchy, layering T-shirt, under a nice button up shirt, a jacket, or a light sweater, or even another T-shirt. Alone, these "stretchy" T-shirts can be much too showy.

President Hinckley lovingly taught us: "Modesty in dress and manner will assist in protecting against temptation. It may be difficult to find modest clothing, but it can be found with enough effort. . . . You can be attractive without being immodest. . . . Draw some rigid parameters, a line in the sand, as it were, beyond which you will not go."[19] It is time to draw our lines in the sand. It is time to say yes to fashions, which will enhance modesty, and to say no to the fads that will erode it.

TEACHING MODESTY

Whether you are a mother, an aunt, or grandmother; whether you are single or married, youthful or not so youthful, modesty is a gospel principle to be followed. It is a principle of protection for *everyone* at any age. Here are some suggestions for those who are "teachers" of the principle of modesty:

1. Start early. Teach the principle of modesty to children at an early age. I started teaching about modesty when my kids were just two years old. I would say things like, "Oh, that is a good choice. Jesus wants us to be modest and that is a modest outfit because . . . ." I remember my second-oldest daughter, Sydney, when she was just three, pointing out a swimsuit at the store and saying, "Mommy, that is not 'mode-est.'" Our children are sponges soaking up whatever we teach them. If you haven't started teaching and preaching modesty, start now. Don't underestimate your influence. Explain why an outfit *is* and *isn't* modest. Children want to know why and, in this situation, the answer "just because" will not teach them the principle. They need to know the doctrine behind modesty—age appropriate, of course.

2. Set the standard early and stick to it. Consistency is key! No matter how young your children are, the standards need to be the same. If you don't want your teenage daughters wearing bikini's, don't let your two-year-old wear them. It might be cute to see the tummy of a toddler in a two-piece and your nine-year-old may not, yet, have a womanly figure, but I guarantee standards will be followed much easier later on if you've been consistent in your standards and teachings early on. If you haven't changed the rules just because body shapes have changed, your children will be more inclined to respect the rules because they've always been the rules. They will have a testimony of the standards as well because you've taught them. In teaching modesty as a Principle of Obedience, it is vital that standards of modesty don't change because of age or circumstance. It is important to keep the standards at all times, and in all things, and in all places, throughout your children's lives. That is the essence of true obedience.

I have friends who have "changed the rules" just because their girls have matured, and they readily admit they have found it much harder to back pedal. If wearing a full-piece swimsuit has always been the standard, there will be no question that it always is and always will be the standard. When children are questioning "why" they can't wear something, don't be afraid to use answers like, "Our family is different" or "We have standards that we follow because . . ." These are good enough reasons to say no to certain styles. Be consistent about what is acceptable in your family and don't be afraid to set boundaries.

As your children mature, encourage them to spend time praying and studying the words of the prophets regarding modesty. Let them do a search on LDS.org for the word *modest* and *immodest*. See what kind of information they find about how they should dress. Let them tell you how they feel about. (This is great family home evening and Young Women's activity.)

3. Model modesty. Be an example of modesty. Do exactly what you preach and teach. We all know that children watch us and they learn from us. Can I say more? If you have ever had the experience looking through a photo album and had one of your children say, "Mommy, is that you? And you're wearing *what*?" That alone is reason enough to model modesty. (And, yes, that happened. And, yes, to those of us to whom it *has* happened and to those of us who have had to explain away the photo from way back when, well, now we can say, "I know better and I do better. And I *am* better because I have a strong testimony of why being modest is so important to the Lord."

4. Make modesty a matter of prayer. Seek the Lord's counsel. Share your desires and concerns with the Lord. He will help you make correct choices and teach correct principles. No matter of virtue is too small for the Lord. Is it silly to pray over a swimsuit or a prom dress? I don't think so. In the Young Women's General Broadcast in March 2008 a group of Young Women and their leaders did, and the Lord answered them. One young woman remarked how surprised she was to find answers so readily in the scriptures. Her testimony and faith grew as a result.

A MODEST SUMMARY

The Lord cares about what we wear, how we wear it, and who we wish to please when we wear it. Why? Because being modest safeguards something He considers to be very sacred—our bodies. Remember, the Lord loves and honors women who adorn themselves in modest apparel, professing godliness with their good works (1 Timothy 2:9–10). What we wear does affect our virtue and the virtue of others. In the words of President David O. McKay: "Are you—a woman—willing to go before your Maker and be judged in the clothes you have on?"[20]

NOTES

1. John S. Tanner, "To Clothe a Temple," *Ensign,* Aug. 1992, 44.
2. Ibid.
3. Ibid.
4. *For the Strength of Youth* (pamphlet, 2001), 14.
5. F. Burton Howard, "Eternal Marriage," *Liahona,* May 2003, 92.
6. Bruce R. McConkie, "The Ten Commandments of Peculiar People," *BYU Speeches,* 28 January 1975.
7. Robert C. Oaks, "Who's on the Lord's Side? Who?" *Ensign,* May 2005, 48.
8. Sheri L. Dew, *If Life Were Easy, It Wouldn't Be Hard* (Salt Lake City: Deseret Book, 2005), 113.
9. *Basic Manual for Priesthood Holders, Part A.* Lesson 19, "Teaching Modesty and Virtue in the Home."
10. Brigham Young, as quoted in Peggy Hawkins, "Fads and Faith," *New Era,* Oct. 1971, 15.
11. *For the Strength of Youth.*
12. Guide to the Scriptures, "Modesty," http://scriptures.lds.org/en/gs/m/41.
13. D. Todd Christofferson, "A Sense of the Sacred," *Liahona,* Jun. 2006, 28. Emphasis added.
14. *For the Strength of Youth.*

15. Dallin H. Oaks, "Pornography," *Liahona*, May 2005.

16. Hawkins, "Fads and Faith."

17. "Image Integrity," *Church News*, 23 Jun. 2007.

18. Judith Rasband, as quoted in "Modesty Matters," *Liahona*, Jun. 2006, 22.

19. Gordon B. Hinckley, "Stay on the High Road," *Ensign*, May 2004, 112.

20. David O. McKay, quoted by Hawkins, "Fads and Faith."

Dear Friend,

I wish we could have this next conversation talking woman-to-woman sitting in the comfort of my living room. We'd laugh about our good hair days and our bad hair days. At some point we'd even feel comfortable enough to talk about the times we have struggled with our body image, because we've all struggled. (I don't know of a woman who hasn't.) In our sharing, we'd find validation in knowing we've both "been there."

We all want to feel good about ourselves and our bodies. Having a positive self-image is important; however, in seeking to feel good about ourselves and our bodies we have to be careful. Why? Because the adversary has masterminded many counterfeit identities which are enticing and appealing to women, and if we're not looking in the right places we could end up exchanging our eternal identity for one of these counterfeits.

I hope as you read these next two chapters you will take time to ponder and listen to the gentle whisperings of the spirit. Please know that I am sharing my thoughts and inspired counsel, from those who have authority, in hopes that young women and women of all ages, will be inspired to love their bodies as God made them and desire to seek after virtuous beauty—the kind of beauty that in the eyes of our Lord and Maker is most beautiful above all.

With love and sisterly friendship—

Jodi

11

The Body Is Sacred and Divine

"In the image of his own body,
male and female, created he them."
—Moses 6:9

One afternoon, while working on this manuscript, I heard the hum of the mail truck pulling out of my circle. I needed a break from writing, so I headed upstairs and out the door to get the mail. Reaching into the mailbox, I pulled out a stack of envelopes. Stuck between the fast food coupons and grocery ads was a clothing catalog. The address label was marked "To Resident." It was something I didn't ordinarily receive. I couldn't help but immediately notice the sexily posed women on the front and back covers. Without even thumbing threw the pages, thoughts began popping into my head like corn kernels in a hot pan of oil. "You don't look as thin as these women. Aren't you feeling a little plumper than usual? Look how perfect their makeup is, and not a hair out of place, unlike your mop that's been held hostage by that claw-clip going on two days now." I furrowed my brow. The silent conversation continued. "Your teeth aren't as white. Your skin's not as smooth. Gee, you're looking old . . . " *STOP!* I jolted myself back to reality. In only a few short seconds, those pictures had an affect on me. And not a very positive one. So what did I do? I ripped that magazine in half (just like I do all the junk mail) and tossed it into the trash! "That is *not* what being a woman is about!" I said out loud as the garbage can lid shut with a bang. I noticed my neighbor's back window was open. I checked to see if perhaps she saw me giving idle threats to my garbage. Thankfully, I was in the clear. I then marched up the driveway, headed back downstairs, sat down at my computer and typed these words: "Satan wants women to believe their self-worth is all tied up in sexuality and physical beauty. And that is a lie!"

Now, I know that is a lie. But come on! I don't know about you, but I can't compete with those "desperate housewives." Deep down I know I shouldn't feel like I have to. But, truthfully, it's hard to measure up to an ideal standard. Especially a standard that isn't even "real." It can be frustrating when all around us are messages (as well as other women) telling us our body isn't "good enough" unless it resembles a supermodel's. (And that can be disheartening considering most gene pools lack "supermodel" DNA.)

Ladies! Images in the media can be like slow poison that sucks us into a worldly view of how a woman's body "should" look. We have to be careful—oh, so very careful as to how much influence we allow the media to have. Elder Jeffrey R. Holland of the Quorum of the Twelve apostles has acknowledged society has been "brutal" with young women and women regarding the way they should look. He has indicated that television, movies, and magazines bombard women and young girls with messages that "looks are everything."[1] This pressure to look a certain way, to have your body look a certain way, and to dress a certain way is *immense*. It causes feelings of inadequacy, inferiority, low self-esteem, self-doubt, and poor body image. It is a real pressure that pushes women and young women (even young girls) to set *idealistic* and *unrealistic* expectations for themselves—giving some reason enough to starve themselves and others to submit to expensive and painful surgeries.

How can we keep ourselves from falling into what I call the "worldly woman identity trap"? For starters, we must recognize who is behind the idealistic and unrealistic propaganda depicting how a woman should look. It's the adversary. And, remember, his "ideal" is *not* the Lord's "ideal." I guarantee you the best thing we can do for our self-esteem, right up front, is to throw these negative messages in the trash—right where they belong!

POWERFUL MEDIA IMAGES DISTORT AND CONFUSE BODY IMAGE

Satan uses the media as a tool to confuse and distort women's (and men's) perceptions about the way a woman should look, how they should dress, and how they should act. These messages seem to be doing exactly what Satan intends them to do—confuse us! Consider this study from February of 2007 by the American Psychological Association. It reveals "an unhealthy sexualization is putting young and adolescent girls increasingly at risk." Dr. Eileen Zurbriggen, head of the task force and associate professor of psychology at the University of California, Santa Cruz, states: "We have ample evidence to conclude that sexualization has negative effects in a variety of domains, including cognitive functioning, physical and mental health, and healthy sexual development." In summary, the study concludes that when the media shows women dressed in provocative and revealing clothing, a message is communicated that *success* comes from being an attractive sexual object. The report also concludes young girls are learning that "presenting oneself as sexually desirable, and thereby gaining the attention of men, is, and should be, the focal goal for women."[2] Sadly, there are many young girls and women who dress and treat their bodies as if this were true.

From magazine covers to flashy billboard signs, to crude and vulgar websites, and provocative TV shows and movies, powerful images communicate that a woman's power lies within her ability to draw attention to herself and to her body. These messages are masterminded by the adversary as part of his master plan of deception. They are for the purpose of clouding our eternal vision. Prophets and apostles have warned that those who buy into Satan's views will eventually lose their eternal focus. Some may even end up selling their birthright for a mess of pottage.

SATAN'S VIEW ON THE BODY

Satan has "sexualized" the body as an object to be worshipped, consumed, gratified, displayed, and exploited. There are no qualms about that. In fact, haven't you noticed how all of Satan's tactics are designed to confuse us about our bodies, their purposes, and their importance? Drugs, alcohol, pornography, immodesty, vanity, immorality, violence—these are all part of Satan's arsenal of weaponry designed to enslave bodies in sin. Why? Why is he so interested in our bodies? Because Satan is jealous. He does not have a physical body and he never will. Joseph Smith taught: "We came to this earth that we might have a body and present it pure before God in the celestial kingdom. The great principle of happiness consists in having a body. The devil has no body, and herein is his punishment."[3]

Imagine how Satan must feel not having a physical body. Think of all the things he *cannot* do because he doesn't have a one. Without a physical body, Satan's progression is thwarted. So, fueled by his misery and jealousy, he desires for us to become miserable like he is (2 Nephi 2:27). So what does he do? He does everything possible to distort eternal truths about the purpose and use of our bodies in hopes that we will fall prey to his deceptions. If you don't think Satan has a plan, think again.

M. Russell Ballard explains Satan's tactics are "to get you so preoccupied with the world's glitzy lie about [who you are] that you completely miss what you have come here to do and to become."[4] And just *who* are we and *what* have we come here to do? We are daughters of God. And we have come here "trailing abilities and assignments from our premortal existence."[5] Part of our mission is to help lead sons and daughters back to our Father in Heaven. Satan knows this. He knows the influence for good the daughters of God can have on all of God's children. And he knows, if *we* become preoccupied with the glitz and the glam and the fads and the fashions then he will have an even greater chance at getting those who follow after us to become preoccupied as well—and maybe even at an earlier age. Elder Richard G. Scott confirms this thought and adds: "Satan has unleashed a seductive campaign to undermine the sanctity of womanhood, to deceive the daughters of God and divert them from their divine destiny."[6] Thus we learn Satan's attack on women is intentional—for even in a little season much is at stake.

THE TRUTH ABOUT OUR BODIES

Through the scriptures and living prophets, God has revealed eternal truths about the purpose, use, and importance of the body. These eternal truths serve as a *protection* against Satan's "emotional deception." They reveal a perspective drastically different than that of the world's. It is important to understand each one of these eternal truths and to gain a testimony of them. They help us transform the vision of our bodies and release our spirits from the worldly views and practices that so heavily weigh us down. Here are some Eternal Truths that will help us in our quest to define our body image as God intended.

1. Our bodies are sacred gifts from God. A gift is something given to someone with love and affection. God gifted our bodies to us in this way. He gave us the gift of a physical body because he loves us and wants us to become like him. To God, a body *is* a sacred gift. Sacred means to "set apart" as something holy. Are you treating your body as the holy and sacred gift it was intended to be? Are you viewing your body in the way God intended you to view it? Are you showing gratitude to God for this precious gift? Our bodies are for the purpose of learning, progressing, serving, and glorifying the giver of the gift: God. Our bodies are not for the purpose of glorifying the self.[7] They are intended to glorify our Creator and to help to bring to pass the immortality and eternal life of mankind.

Satan's view of the body is all about glorifying self. When we think we "deserve" to look a certain way, we are doing exactly what Satan wants us to do—looking at our bodies, not as sacred gifts, but as objects. Objects that can be manipulated, adorned, and dressed any way that is pleasing to one's self. "Deserving" to look a certain way is not glorifying our Maker—it is clearly an issue of unrighteous entitlement. Trifling with a sacred gift such as one's physical body is as if we have accepted a sacred gift in vain. "The scriptures warn us not to trifle with sacred things and to be wary of treating the body disrespectfully. Alma asks, 'Can ye lay aside these things, and trample the Holy One under your feet; yea, can ye be puffed up in the pride of your hearts . . . setting your hearts upon the vain things of the world?'. . . Such scriptures beg us to consider how we regard our bodies?"[8]

It is wise to consider these questions: "If you become preoccupied with manipulating or adorning your body, for what purpose are you using your gift? If you do not properly care for your body, to what extent are you limiting your gift? If you use your body in direct opposition to the commandments of God, what ends will your gift serve?"[9] These poignant questions have helped me as I have defined what is proper treatment for my body. They have guided me as I have studied, pondered, prayed, and fasted to know the Lord's will concerning my gift. I hope these questions will help you, too. In summary, the only way to truly be happy is to honor God and the gift He gave us. We do that by accepting our bodies (imperfections and all) and treating them as sacred and divine.

2. Our bodies are made in the image of God. We read in the Pearl of Great Price "in the image of his own body, male and female, created he them" (Moses 6:9). From this we learn we are more like God because we are embodied. "Our religion stands virtually alone in believing that God has a tangible body of flesh and bone and that our bodies were literally created in His likeness."[10] Our prophet, President Thomas S. Monson has said: "God our father has ears with which to hear our prayers. He has eyes with which to see our actions. He has a mouth with which to speak to us. He has a heart with which to feel compassion and love. He is real. He is living. We are his children made in his image. We look like him and he looks like us."[11] This eternal truth should give us reason enough to love our bodies; to respect our bodies, and to treat our bodies as sacred and holy, for we *are* the "workmanship" of God's hands (Moses 7:32).

Is God beautiful? I believe so. Joseph Smith described God's beauty as a "brightness and glory [that defies] all description" (Joseph Smith History—1:17). So, if there are no words and no description adequate enough to explain the exquisiteness of God's beauty then I can scarcely imagine how beautiful He really must be. But as I imagine God's beauty, I realize His beauty has nothing to do with beauty in the way that the world defines it; for God's beauty—beauty that defies all description—has to do with the "beauty of holiness" (1 Chronicles 16:29). Holiness is eternal beauty and that is why, I believe, it defies all description. We must come to know and embrace this eternal truth: to be made in the image of God is beautiful because it is holy.

3. Our bodies are mortal houses for our eternal spirits. Our bodies complete our spirits. In Doctrine and Covenants 88:15, we are taught "the spirit and the body are the soul of man." Without a body, our spirits cannot progress. Being wise stewards over our bodies allows our spirits to learn, progress, serve, and glorify God. Myriads of Satan's entrapments imprison the body physically and mentally, resulting in spiritual bondage. Just think of a body that is enslaved in addiction. The spirit inside that body is literally imprisoned. Its use of agency is limited. It cannot progress. A mortal body can be controlled by indulgences such as overeating, not eating enough, pornography, or chasing after vanity—this is what the scriptures mean when they refer to bondage. Such worldly practices, as well as many others, control the physical body and thus hinder the growth of the spirit. Whatever affects the physical also affects the spiritual and visa versa. Through the power of the Atonement one can *free* oneself from the tyranny of these worldly practices. In making choices that protect our mortal body, we protect our eternal spirit; thus we are able to receive God's blessings from on high in their fullest.

4. Gender is eternal. The Proclamation to the World on the Family reminds us that gender is eternal. As intelligences we were female and male and our spirits carried that identity into mortality. Our gender gives us an identity that will follow us into the hereafter and beyond. Because of our gender we are responsible for fulfilling specific assignments here on earth–assignments that will follow us into the eternities. The prophets have taught that if we are faithful to our gender roles, we will find joy not only here in this life but in the hereafter and beyond. President Holland states: "I want you to be proud you are a woman. I want you to feel the reality of what that means, to know who you truly are. . . . A woman, including a young woman, occupies a majesty all her own in the divine design of the Creator. You are, as Elder James E. Talmage once phrased it, 'a sanctified investiture which none shall dare profane.' "[12]

5. Our bodies are temples. Temples all over the world are well-known for their architectural beauty. Each one is distinctly beautiful in its own right. But, although temples are beautiful on the outside, they are most precious and unique because of what happens on the inside. Sacred ordinances and covenants learned in the temple give patrons the necessary keys to someday return to God's presence. Our bodies are similar to temples in this way. "The worth of the body is great in the sight of God, but the preciousness of the body comes from what it allows us to learn and do."[13] Our bodies may radiate a beauty on the outside, but they are most beautiful when serving as an instrument of God and fulfilling heavenly purposes.

BE A FAITHFUL STEWARD OF YOUR BODY

In my speaking engagements, I have been asked over and over, "Is it vain to take care of our bodies?" Absolutely not! The Word of Wisdom requires us to be faithful stewards over our bodies. Doing so affords us the blessings in Doctrine and Covenants 89 that we shall run and not be weary and walk and not faint. We should eat healthy and be as physically fit as we can be. Fulfilling daily responsibilities become challenging tasks if our bodies are not healthy and strong. Strong bodies are needed in order to accomplish whatever the Lord expects of us. That makes perfect sense. Approaching forty, and having a three-year-old rule the household, rummaging through drawers and emptying out their contents faster than I can keep up reminds me of how physically demanding raising little ones can be. (Seriously, I need a nap!)

Having a healthy and physically fit body is truly a gift. My family and I enjoy going on hikes and I know I would not enjoy them nearly as much if I were not in good physical shape. Proper nutrition, sleep, and exercise help us safeguard our physical body and allows us to enjoy life more fully. These practices help us achieve balance.

CARE FOR YOUR BODY IN BALANCE

As I mentioned, my family enjoys going on hikes. One place we visit each year is Arches National Park in Southern Utah. One of the amazing wonders in the park is Balanced Rock—it is a boulder, the size of a house, literally balancing on top of a rock one quarter of its size. Although the boulder is tilted to one side, miraculously it is still balanced. One day erosion, wind, and rain will eventually wear down the base of Balanced Rock and the boulder will fall. No one knows exactly when that will occur. Only nature knows.

What I learned from studying Balanced Rock was this: balance makes even the most precarious situations possible. The environment we live in is precarious. Demanding schedules exhaust our energy; trials and tribulations drain our emotional reserves. But finding time to take care of our physical bodies, although challenging, is so very necessary. Balance is achieved by devoting adequate time to eating, sleeping, and exercising. Doing these things will enhance our physical capabilities, improve our emotional well-being, and boost our vitality and health; thus allowing us to accomplish our responsibilities, goals, and challenges with greater ease.

As with all things in life, it is important to be moderate in anything we pursue. Just as neglecting our body leads to an imbalance, so does a narrow focus and passionate pursuit of physical "perfection." Careful introspection will help us determine if pursuits to care for our physical bodies are in balance with the bounds the Lord has set. Being attune to the promptings of the Holy Ghost will help us adjust our routines to achieve proper balance—balance which will help us achieve inner peace.

EAT, BREATHE, AND MOVE

Let me suggest a formula I have used over the years to improve my physical health: eat, breathe, and move. Simple enough? Eat enough good foods to fuel your body; breathe deeply to manage stress; and last but not least—*move*. Whether it's walking, running, jazzercising, kickboxing, cross-training, hiking, jump-roping, dancing . . . just *move*! Our routines don't have to be complicated and take hours each day. A simple focus on eating right, breathing and relaxing, and moving can improve your overall physical health. One article I read said you can improve your physical health just by exercising long enough to break a sweat at least once each day. This is a guaranteed great place to start on the road to better physical health.

Focusing on Optimal Health Not Optimal Size

In studying the scriptures, conference talks, Church magazines, and other Church curriculum, not once have I found any reference calling for women to be "perfect" physically. (Especially not perfect by worldly standards.) I have found no scripture, talk, lesson, quote, or otherwise, from prophets, church leaders, or respected women of faith saying, "We need women who have washboard stomachs and 18" waistlines (not to mention perky and busting bust lines). Nowhere did I find references saying, "We need women who can lose ten pounds in ten hours and women who are sixty but who look like twenty." Not in the least. In researching this book, I have only found references from our prophets and Church leaders pleading with us, and counseling us, to be healthy in mind, body, and spirit; and to be "more accepting" of ourselves and the bodies that God gave to us.[14] Over and over, I have found gentle reminders that true beauty comes from having Christ's image radiating in our countenances (Alma 5:14) and not from being a size 2.

Be Grateful for the Wonderful Body that is Yours

We should be forever grateful for the blessing of having a body—especially a body that is blessed to function properly. In Psalms 24:4, the Lord says He stands by "[s]he that hath clean hands, and a pure heart; who hath not lifted up [her] soul unto vanity." When I read this scripture, I think of some of God's children who are born with mental and physical challenges, which limit the proper functioning of their physical bodies. These individuals have much to teach us. The following experience told to me by my girlfriend illustrates this perfectly.

> I was attending a session at the temple and in that session happened to be a man who was suffering from a degenerative muscle disease. Because of his disease, this man could not control his arms, legs, head, or face. Throughout the session, his arms flailed, his head jerked, and his body contorted. It took three temple workers to help him dress. As far as bodies go, this man didn't have an ideal one, but his mind was sharp and intellectually he understood everything that was taking place. He didn't limit his abilities by the limitations placed on him by his physical body. He was focused on being in the house of the Lord,

making covenants and blessing those on the other side of the veil.

As the session came to a close, I caught the eye of this man. He smiled at me a long smile. I wish I could have expressed to him how deeply his presence affected me. This man had not one ounce of vanity. He only had humility. If only I could have seen his soul.

The intricacies of our bodies are miraculous and amazing! Actually they're phenomenal! President Hinckley said, "These remarkable and wonderful bodies are [God's] handiwork."[15] I remind myself of this often. Whenever I become frustrated with my "less-than-perfect" body, I center my soul on gratitude. I focus on the innumerable blessings my body provides like having legs that allow me to walk; arms that allow me to hug and hold my little children. I am grateful for eyes that allow me to see the beauty of this earth. I am grateful for ears that allow me to listen to birds singing in the peach trees in my backyard; for working organs that perform their bodily functions in the way that they should so I can clean my house, drive a car, ride a bike, make dinner, play with my children, and take care of my family. I'm so grateful for a heart that beats, blood that flows, and fingers that can type. (At this moment, I happen to be overly grateful for eyelashes because for some reason mine seem to be falling out by the dozens! I'm sure it's the stress of this book! Breathe, Jodi, breathe.) I am grateful to have a physical body that has given birth to four beautiful children and has recovered from illnesses without lasting effects. Simple acts, such as buttering toast or fluffing a pillow, become tiny miracles when you consider the intricacies of the human body. Some days I can scarcely consider all that I have been given physically—blessings that have nothing to do with my body's shape or size.

I hope and pray each one of us will strengthen our testimony of the purpose and importance of the sacred gift that is our body and then, by example, show our daughters (and our sons) what it means to be grateful, forever grateful, for the miraculous handiwork God created for us; for it will be our example that will be our children's best teacher.

THE BODY AS A LIVING SACRIFICE

The Apostle Paul told the saints to present their bodies as living sacrifices before the Lord saying: "I beseech you . . . by the mercies of God, that ye present your bodies a *living sacrifice, holy,* acceptable unto God, which is your reasonable service. And be not conformed to this world: but be ye transformed by the renewing of your mind, that ye may prove what *is* that good, and acceptable, and perfect, will of God" (Romans 12:1–2; empasis added).

What does it mean to present our bodies as living sacrifices to Jesus Christ? I look at it this way; it is the least that we can do for all he has done for us. He has given us, through the Atonement, the unimaginable gift of the Resurrection. He has rescued us from physical and spiritual death, making it possible for our bodies and spirits to reunite. He has atoned for our sins and made it possible for us to live again with our Heavenly Father. Christ sacrificed all . . . giving his very life for us. The very least we can do is sacrifice for Him. That's all he asks of us; to come out of the world and follow him.

Becoming living sacrifices means we give up something worldly to gain something heavenly. "For some, such an offering may include giving up a quest to become model-thin, while for others, it may include giving up excessive grooming habits and the wearing of costly or immodest apparel. For still others, it may include giving up the short-term pleasures of over-eating, the avoidance of proper exercise, or the viewing of others' bodies as objects for self-gratification. With such forsaking of worldly practices comes tremendous spiritual gains."[16] Making our bodies as living sacrifices, means we give everything we are physically and spiritually to God. We forgo having a perfect body in this life to receive a glorified body in the next. We offer to God our might, mind, and strength, and transform ourselves by becoming spiritually reborn through the power of the Holy Ghost. To become living sacrifices, we sacrifice; that is how we become beautiful like God.

SACRIFICE OF THE CHILDBEARING BODY

When I think of making sacrifices I can't help but think of bearing children. Each time a woman becomes pregnant she becomes a co-creator with God to bring to pass the immortality and eternal life of man. In pregnancy, a woman shares her body with another human being. She basically rents out her womb so another mortal body can form within her. As the baby's body grows, the woman's body transforms. Her shape changes. Her belly bulges. Her feet swell. Her organs become misplaced as the baby runs out of space to grow. Although her body may never return to its original starting point, a mother-to-be sacrifices anyway—because she knows without her gift, there would be no new life.

The creation process of a newly formed life is miraculous to say the very least. Each trip to the doctor verifies this truth. As a heartbeat sounds on the monitor, and as tiny legs, hands, fingers, and toes are all accounted for on the ultrasound a mother's heart leaps for joy. Although, the birthing process is painful, I dare say I have never heard a woman say it wasn't worth it.

After birth, women are often left with stretch marks, dimples, sags, and droops, and in some cases "belly Jell-O" that just won't go away no matter how many sit-ups are performed. But these imperfections are sacred marks; signs of a great sacrifice. These marks are not to make us superior in any way over women who have not physically born children. But, too often, the childbearing body is looked down upon. Women of virtue mustn't let that be the case; for childbearing is a noble endeavor sanctioned by God. Let us view stretch marks and misplaced body parts as sacred marks; reminders of a glorious time when the spiritual converged with the temporal, creating a miracle of the divine. Being co-creators with God shouldn't create in us pride, but should fill us with deep humility because, by the power of God, the miracle of life emerged through us.

In plain speaking, if we define our bodies by what is no longer perky and what is no longer firm, we are missing the boat! Miracles of life happen because a mother's body becomes a living sacrifice. And if our concern is such that we don't look the same in a bathing suit because we've had children, we are simply focusing on the wrong things.

AGING GRACEFULLY

Once an elderly woman was asked to give some advice on aging to a group of younger women in their thirties and forties. She stood at the podium and remarked, "I'm ninety-years-young and I've been told I have some advice to share." Looking out at the thirty-something crowd, she said, "All of this fuss over having a perfect body is nonsense. But at ninety years of age, I must say, I'm thrilled to say I'm closer to getting one than you are!" This is a clever way to look at aging.

There is a place that gives me a unique perspective on aging—a place where I feel ageless—the temple. Perhaps, it is because, in the temple, I can touch eternity. When I visit the temple, I see many silvery-haired sisters and brothers busily engaged in doing the work of the Lord, and they are smiling and looking so content. I think, "These are happy people!" And they are! But how could that be? In reality they probably have more aches than they'd like to have. They may be slower than they used to be. Their eyes and ears don't work as they once did. And yet, they smile as if they are having the best day of their lives. What's their secret? All dressed in white, they are united in purpose. They are focused on what is important. They are busily engaged in the Lord's work. That is their secret to happiness.

It is in the temple I receive a witness that, although my body is temporal, my spirit is not of this world. In that celestial setting, I am reminded to look forward to the day when my body will be perfected. Not perfected in the way the world interprets it to mean. It doesn't mean we're going to look like supermodels and incredible hulks. That's not how the Lord defines perfection. The scriptures teach us that the Lord's definition of a "perfected" body is a "glorified" body, which is the uniting of the body and spirit for eternity. Yes, mortal aches and pains, effects of aging, and handicaps will no longer exist, and every single hair on our heads will be accounted for. But a "perfected" body lies within our divine potential to become perfected in Christ and not necessarily perfected in a "physical" sense as one might think. That may not be what the magazines are selling. But *that* is eternal truth. And *that* is what's real.

NOTES

1. Holland, "To Young Women."
2. Catholic News, "The Sexualization of Girls," http://www.catholic.org.sg/cn/wordpress/?p=1453.
3. Joseph Smith as quoted in Boyd K. Packer, "Ye Are the temple of God." *Ensign*, Nov. 2000, 72.
4. M. Russell Ballard, "Women of Righteousness," *Ensign*, Apr. 2002, 66.
5. Nelson, "For Such a Time as This."
6. Richard G. Scott, "The Sanctity of Womanhood," *Ensign*, May 2000, 36.
7. Diane L. Spangler, "The Body, a Sacred Gift." *Ensign*, Jul. 2005, 14.
8. Ibid.
9. Ibid.
10. Ibid.
11. Thomas S. Monson, as quoted in" All Human Beings Are Created in the Image of God," *Liahona*, Jul. 2008, 25.
12. Holland, "To Young Women."
13. Spangler, "The Body, a Sacred Gift."
14. Holland, "To Young Women."
15. Gordon B. Hinckley, "The Scourge of Illicit Drugs," *Ensign*, Nov. 1989, 48.
16. Spangler, "The Body, a Sacred Gift."

12

Walking Away from Vanity

WHY HAVE THEY PROVOKED ME TO ANGER WITH THEIR GRAVEN IMAGES,
AND WITH STRANGE VANITIES?
—Jeremiah 8:19

One of the biggest challenges facing modern women of today is vanity. Vanity is the antithesis of virtue. Everything in God's plan of happiness has its opposite, and there is purpose in this opposition. That purpose is to test us. To see if what we say really matters to us *really* does. And vanity is for purpose of testing our virtue: it is to test the *strength* of our virtue.

Why vanity? Satan knows he can't tempt us with certain things because, for women of faith, there are some things that just aren't tempting. Like taking drugs—not even interested. So, to me that's not a real temptation. But vanity? Looking a certain way. Wearing certain clothes. Having a certain lifestyle. For many of us, these are temptations, so that's where Satan concentrates his efforts.

In the Bible Dictionary vanity is equated with falsehood and deceit. It is synonymous with the words empty, transitory, and fleeting (Bible Dictionary, King James Version). Ecclesiastes 1:7 states: "All the rivers run into the sea; yet the sea is not full." Simply put, vanity is a sea that is never full. An individual operating in vanity-mode fails to fill the ocean within no matter what is done to fill it. A vain individual is left wanting, needing, expecting, and desiring . . . *more*. But one might ask how could this be? How could one be spending time, money, and resources seeking to be happy, and, yet, not *be* happy? It's actually pretty simple. The answer

127

relates back to the definition of vanity. Vanity is empty and a well cannot be filled with emptiness.

Vanity can affect any one of us. The fall of Adam made all women susceptible to natural woman tendencies and one of these tendencies is to become vain. Many references in the scriptures pertain to vanity. Here are a just a few.

- Ecclesiastes 6:2—"*Vanity* . . . is an evil disease."
- Ecclesiastes 5:10—"He that loveth silver shall not be satisfied with silver."
- 2 Kings 17:15— "And they rejected [Christ's] statutes, and his covenant . . . and they followed *vanity*, and became *vain*."
- Psalms 4:2 "O, ye [daughters] of men. . . how long will ye love *vanity*?"
- Jeremiah 8:19—"Why have they provoked me to anger with their graven images, and with strange *vanities*?"

STRANGE VANITIES

Recently, while on a family vacation, I was watching a television show about brides. A commercial aired that basically said the following: "Hey, you want to look your best for your wedding day, right? So . . ." And I'm thinking the commercial is going to say something like, "So, check out the dresses at Dresses Are Us. Or, "Get that perfect up-do at Hair-Aramma." But no! This commercial basically said, "To look perfect for that perfect day be sure to surgically fix those droopy eyelids, get a tuck for that tummy flab, and while you're at it, laser off that unwanted jiggle." (I think I needed a chin implant after watching that commercial because mine dropped to the floor.) Here I am, picturing this darling (not to mention twenty-something and beautiful) college co-ed saying, "Oh, my dear fiancée, we have to set a date six weeks after my surgery date so that the redness from my eyelid lift, and the soreness from my tummy tuck won't be an issue on our wedding night." Ladies, eighteen years ago when I got married, the only advertisement I remember was for strawberry crepes, and we served them at my reception! We have seriously landed on Planet Makeover. And nothing is *not* makeover-able. This is more than just "airtime." It's a dangerous trend pushing women away from the paths of virtue and closer to vanity.

Many surgeries and medical procedures can produce miracles. But these miracles I'm referring to have nothing to do with vanity. I once watched a television show about a doctor who created a new ear for a young woman who was born without one. I know of doctors who spend their own money and time traveling to third-world countries to operate on children born with cleft pallets and debilitating physical deformities, children whose lives would be considerably wrought with hardship without these precious, life-changing surgeries. Two times in the past year, I have watched television updates about conjoined twins being surgically separated, so they can live as two separate human beings with bodies of their own. At eighty-three years old, my maternal grandmother received a new hip to help her walk without pain. A dear friend of mine has undergone several jaw reconstruction surgeries after a tumor was discovered in her jawbone. Doctors even had the technology to record the way she ate, chewed, swallowed, and talked, so they could reconstruct her face exactly and not risk changing the way she performed those functions. Incredible! These are examples of just some of the wonderful, miraculous uses, and wise purposes of surgery. But what about surgery for vanity's sake? Should we be traveling on the highway of vanity in search of the "ideal" body just because we *can*? Just because technology is available to us? Just because we want to look a certain way?

Choosing Virtue over Vanity on the Highway of Vanity

Now, I'm not going to pretend and say I don't I know what a "good hair day" feels like; and I'm certainly *not* going to fib and tell you looking beautiful doesn't interest me. I'm a woman living in the twenty-first century, and I know the pull of worldly glamour is strong (especially when the pull of gravity seems to be taking over my body). But, my dear sisters, the road to vanity is an ever-winding freeway with multiple lane changes and no speed limits. Once we're on the highway of vanity, at which exit do we choose to get off? And are we so naive in our thinking that getting off an exit will be as simple as turning on our blinker and driving away?

With each step taken on the road of vanity, we step further and further away from virtue. And let's not deceive ourselves into thinking there is safety in driving along the country roads. Eventually those roads hook into big city highways. Really, the only way to be safe is to walk in the pedestrian lane and avoid driving on the highway of vanity all together.

Seeking Guidance from Scriptures and Church Leaders

So how we do we make decisions in the age of botox and tummy tucks? The scriptures teach us the proper use of the body is "to be used, with judgment, not to excess, neither by extortion" (D&C 59:20). This one principle of truth sets a standard, which we should follow as we navigate the highway of physical beauty. It is the standard by which we achieve happiness. Former Young Women's General President Susan W. Tanner taught: "The body must not be twisted [against] the divinely ordained purposes for which [it was] given . . . it must not become our god. . . . Happiness comes from accepting the bodies we have been given as divine gifts and enhancing our natural attributes, not from remaking our bodies after the image of the world. The Lord wants us to be made over—but in His image.[1]

A special witness of Jesus Christ also shared some important counsel on the pursuit of physical beauty in General Conference 2005. Elder Jeffrey R. Holland, Quorum of the Twelve Apostles stated: "In too many cases too much is being done to the human body to meet . . . a fictional (to say nothing of superficial) standard. . . . May you let the eternal realities of the gospel of Jesus Christ lift you above temporal concerns."[2] Is it really possible to be lifted above concerns and insecurities regarding our imperfect bustlines, waistlines, and age lines? Yes, through the power of Jesus Christ we can be lifted above them. Absolutely, yes, we can be! If we will turn to Christ in our desires; if we will turn to him and turn our will over to him, He will heal us. And *healing* is what we need. The Lord will secure our insecurities, calm our concerns, and heal our hearts, even when it comes to how we feel about our "imperfect" bodies. He will replace our anxieties with contentment and peace, if we allow Him to do so. Through the Atonement, Christ will help us see our bodies in a new light and even help us love them with astounding acceptance! This I promise!

How do I know this? Because I've been there. I've experienced it. There have been times I have fallen to my knees asking for relief from my temporal worries and anxieties about my "less-than-perfect" body and I testify I *did* receive healing. My fears, my worries, and my insecurities have been eased through the power of the Lord. My desires for vanity have lessened and I am so much happier because of it.

BLESSINGS AND PROTECTION

Elder Holland, in the previously mentioned counsel, gave an important promise to those who follow the Lord's way. And I bring this up particularly because so many women miss it. He states: "For you to fully claim Heavenly Father's *blessings* and *protection*, we ask you to stay true to the standards of the gospel of Jesus Christ . . . . The Church will always declare standards and will always teach principles . . . [but] our standards are not socially negotiable."[3]

Most people I have talked to seem to skip right over two words: "blessings and protection." However, in these two words are incredible power! What a wonderful motivator to stay true to the standards! You want blessings, don't you? You want protection, don't you? The promise is you'll have them *if* you stay true to the standards. For those who do stay true, these blessings and protection are theirs. But to those who choose *not* to follow this counsel, it is a warning. Promised blessings of protection may be missed when standards and principles are not followed.

President Holland continues:

> In terms of preoccupation with self and a fixation on the physical, this is more than social insanity; *it is spiritually destructive,* and it accounts for much of the unhappiness women, including young women, face in the modern world. And if adults are preoccupied with appearance—tucking and nipping and implanting and remodeling everything that can be remodeled—those pressures and anxieties will certainly seep through to children . . . the problem becomes what the Book of Mormon called "vain imaginations." And in secular society both vanity *and* imagination run wild.[4]

Elder Holland refers to a "preoccupation" with the physical. What is a preoccupation? *Preoccupation* is defined as a concern, a worry, or an anxiety. A preoccupation is not an obsession; surprisingly, to be spiritually destructive, it doesn't have to go that deep. Why would Elder Holland warn us that it is spiritually destructive to be preoccupied with physical appearance? Perhaps one reason is it can easily distract us from what matters most. And isn't that exactly what Satan wants? He wants to distract us long enough to turn our head away from the things of God. Another reason to stay away from "preoccupations" with physical perfection is the affect it has on others—especially children. Elder Holland teaches that when adults are preoccupied (meaning concerned, worried, or anxious) with physical appearance, pressures, and anxieties "seep down" to the children.

Seeing women walk the path of vanity has caused me to wonder, "In choosing what you are choosing, what you are teaching your daughters, and better yet, what are you teaching your sons?" I believe on this one point alone is where virtuous women will make their mark. For the sake of the children, and our children's children, virtuous women who love the Lord will choose to walk away from vain imaginations. They will simply choose a better way.

FOOTPRINTS IN THE SAND

My children and I enjoy making footprints in the sand along the beach of our favorite mountain lake. As we make our sandy prints in the wet sand, our walk often turns into a game to see whose footprints fit more perfectly into my sandy prints. In an eternal sense, I often think of my sandy footprints, with smaller imprints inside them, where my children have placed their feet inside my steps. My little ones aren't just following in my steps, they are actually stepping *in* my steps. Each of us is leaving an eternal footprint for our children and others to follow.

When it comes to the pursuit of physical beauty, my daughters, your daughters, and young women all over the world are learning to love themselves and the bodies that God gave to them. They are looking to us, the women of the Church, to show them the way. They are following our footprints in the sand. They are looking to us to see what we choose and why we choose what we choose. They are watching to see if we will choose virtue or vanity. At President Hinckley's funeral, Elder Earl C. Tingey read this poem by Henry Wadsworth Longfellow:

> Lives of great men [and women] all remind us,
> We can make our lives sublime,
> And, departing, leave behind us
> Footprints on the sands of time.[5]

Our footprints in the sands of time *will* influence generations of girls who will someday have daughters and granddaughters of their own. If we become too comfortable chasing after vain imaginations, these wonderful daughters of God will do the same.

Let us show the daughters of God the virtue of virtues and not the vanity of our vanities. Let us teach our children that our bodies are sacred gifts from God. That they are holy temples for the purpose of helping us grow and progress and not for our own self-gratification. And most important, let us teach our daughters (and sons) to love God and not to love the world. "Love not the world, neither the things that are in the world. If any [woman] love the world, the love of the Father is not in him" (1 John 2:15).

Is There a "Thin Line" Between Virtue and Vanity?

I've heard many times: "There is a thin line between virtue and vanity. It's a hard line to walk, so you just have to be careful." Sisters, this is where we have to uncover the adversary's deceptions. Is there a thin line between virtue and vanity? It depends from whose perspective you're looking. If you're looking from the adversary's perspective, yes. If you're looking from the Lord's perspective, then no. When I prayed, read the scriptures, and fasted to know if there was such a thing as a "thin line" between virtue and vanity, I was lead to the story of Lehi's dream. This was my answer.

Learning about Virtue and Vanity from Lehi's Dream

Picture in your mind a painting of Lehi's dream. There are four groups of people in this painting. In group one, people are firmly holding onto the rod, looking toward the tree of life. These people are willing to sacrifice worldly rewards for eternal rewards. Their grasp is firm and their eyes are looking straight at the tree of life. They are not wandering toward the things of the world. They are not even turning their heads toward the things of the world. They are holding fast to the iron rod with their eyes single to the glory of God.

In group two the people are holding onto the rod, but loosening their grip as they turn their heads toward the big and spacious building and the mists of darkness. Although, they are holding onto the iron rod, they seem intrigued by what the world has to offer them. For now, they continue to hold onto the rod.

Group three consists of the people who have clearly let go of the rod and who are wandering in the "great mists of darkness."

What will happen to the people in groups two and three? Many will eventually make their way to the big and spacious building. Without a firm grasp on the rod, they will not be able to withstand the pressures of the world. They will let go of the rod (for what they think is just a quick tour of the valley) and find themselves wandering in the mists of darkness. Soon, they will give in to temptation. Perhaps some will make their way back to the iron rod, and I hope they will. But choosing to let go of the rod and openly accepting the entreaties of the world subjects them to the influences of the adversary. Before coming back to the rod, they will have to change their hearts and repent.

Finally, let's look at group four. This is a group of people who live in the big and spacious building. These individuals' hearts are converted to the things of the world. They are enjoying their stay at the Big and Spacious Inn. A few of them are looking out the windows mocking those who are holding faithful to the rod. But there are also a handful of others who are looking across the divide with confused looks on their faces. Perhaps they are wondering if they have let go of something valuable, yet they are not willing to give up their suites in the spacious building and go back to the iron rod.

Do you see a "thin line" anywhere in this painting you're envisioning? I don't see one. Where the dark mists are I only see darkness and clouds that make any line, path, or walkway seem obsolete. Lehi even describes the mists as "an exceedingly great mist of darkness." Nephi defines these great mists as "temptations of the devil, which blindeth the eyes, and hardeneth the hearts of the children of men, and leadeth them away into broad roads, that they perish and are lost" (1 Nephi 12:17). Broad roads are certainly not "thin lines."

Now, let's determine the distance between groups one and four: Group one consisted of people holding firmly onto the iron rod and Group Four consisted of people who live in the big and spacious building. How far is the distance between these two groups? If you're imagining the painting correctly, the division between the iron rod and the big and spacious building is *not* just inches, or feet, or a couple of yards away. The individuals in the big and spacious building are clearly off in the distance from the iron rod. The building dwellers aren't even within reaching space of the rod. The point is: there is no thin line between the iron rod and the big and spacious building, and there is no thin line floating around in the great mists of darkness. And, there *isn't* a thin line between virtue and vanity. There is actually a deep crevasse miles wide—a chasm, a moat, a grand canyon, if you will.

"The soul attracts that which it secretly harbors; that which it loves, and also that which it fears; it reaches the height of its cherished aspirations; it falls to the level of its unchastened desires."[6] Hiding vanity is hard to do. We cannot profess to love virtue, but secretly love vanity. We will become what we love and if we love vanity, we will surely become vain.

RULES BEFORE EXCEPTIONS

President Boyd K. Packer, while speaking at Women's Conference in 2006 told this story. He explained of a situation when Sister Belle Spafford was serving as president of the General Relief Society. Sister Spafford was giving counsel to the Relief Society board on the order of things and one of the sisters spoke up and said: "That doesn't fit us. We're an exception! We *are* the exception!" President Packer said Sister Belle responded to this sister's concern by saying: "Dear sister, we'd like not to take care of the exception first. We will take care of the rule first, and then we will see to the exception." President Packer told Sister Spafford that he would be "quoting her all over the world." And he said that he has done just that.[7]

Sometimes we are much too quick to look for reasons to be the "exception" rather than looking for a reason to adhere to the rule. We have been given counsel on the pursuit of physical beauty. So before we consider ourselves to be the exception, we ought to seek the Lord's counsel through study and prayer, sincerely desiring to bend our will toward the Lord's rather than fighting to bend His will to ours.

ACCEPT WHAT WE HAVE AS GOOD ENOUGH AND MORE

In speaking to the sisters at Women's Conference in 2006, Patricia Holland, wife of Jeffrey R. Holland of the Quorum of the Twelve Apostles, stated that "Satan's demonic chant" is forever telling women that what they have is *not* enough. She added, "It is not true! We are more intelligent than this. We are stronger, much stronger, than this! . . . Let us strip ourselves of pride and vanity and envy forever. . . . We have to walk away from these things, but this will not be easy to do."[8]

Why do you think Sister Holland would say walking away from the vain things of the world would not be easy to do? She, too, knows the pull of the world is a real and powerful force—one that, at times, is impossible to ignore. The natural woman in each of us can be persuasive and compelling. But we must remember that the grace of God is stronger than anything the adversary has to offer. Women need the power of God's priesthood and the atoning mercy of the Savior to combat pride and defeat vanity.

WHERE VANITY LIVES INSIDE US: THE PARABLE OF THE SHOES

Before we can strip ourselves of vanity, we have to recognize where inside us vanity lives. Yes, we all have vanity. And we will most likely spend a lifetime trying to purge ourselves of it if we want to return to our Father in Heaven. But know this: recognizing vanity lives within us shouldn't discourage us but make us aware so that we can overcome it.

One might ask at exactly what moment does a virtuous desire turn vain? My vanity and shoe theory may help illustrate this point. When each of my three daughters were about two years old, they developed a fancy for shoes. "Shoosies," they would say. "Pretty shoosies." They would spend hours trying on their shoes, my shoes, and anyone else's shoes that were left by my front door. Whenever we were out shopping, my daughters would get so excited when they would see shoes! Clearly, they were victims of a shoe obsession! It was all quite innocent, but their attraction to shoes was very real and at times very focused.

My young daughters' love of shoes certainly was not vain. (Obviously, a two-year-old cannot be guilty of vanity.) But let's pretend for a moment that at some point my daughters grew older, gained knowledge, and became accountable for their choices, but they became *so focused* on shoes that much of their time and hard-earned money was spent in the pursuit of acquiring shoes. They had to have pink shoes, brown shoes, black shoes, blue shoes, orange shoes, shoes with tassels, shoes with bows, shoes with sparkles, jewels, bells, and bobbles; shoes made of satin, shoes made of lace; rubber shoes, leather shoes, sandals, open-toed shoes, closed-toed shoes; slip-ons, tie-ons, and on and on and on. Shoes, shoes, and more shoes! And all the while, there were some children in the neighborhood that had no shoes to wear. Their innocent love of beautiful shoes had turned to a love of vanity.

At which pair of shoes did their love of shoes turn vain? The answer can only be found inside my daughters' hearts. Shoes are not in and of themselves vain. But shoes, or any other object, passion, possession, or desire, *can* become a source of vanity. Virtue turns to vanity when one's desires become "foolish imaginations of the heart." Our Heavenly Father does not want the "shoes" in our lives (whatever our "shoes" may be) to become foolish imaginations that cause us to lose our place in eternity—not for shoes or anything else for that matter.

THREE STEPS TO OVERCOMING VANITY

When we begin to feel a tinge of vanity seeping into our hearts, there are three things we can do: (1) offer a prayer of gratitude; (2) utilize the healing powers of the Atonement; and (3) go and serve someone. Yes, I'll admit, these sound just like the Sunday School answers. And they are. But they are tried and true.

1. Prayers of Gratitude. Have you ever realized that you can't feel vanity at the same time you feel gratitude? It's just impossible. As we journey toward virtue and away from vanity, gratitude becomes a source of great strength. Saying a prayer full of thanksgiving for every blessing we can think of will immediately soften our hearts and fine-tune our spirits. As we show gratitude for the blessings in our lives, our spiritual ears will hearken to the gentle whisperings of the Holy Spirit. God will speak to us through the Holy Ghost, and our hearts will become humble, more willing to accept the Lord's will. Through prayer, we gain humility which then opens the door to the healing influence of the Spirit and the power of the Savior's atonement.

2. The Atonement. Whatever we feel is broken, whatever we feel is lacking, whatever we feel is inferior, the Savior can heal and make whole. Through the power of God's priesthood, the Lord will turn what we have into enough and show us more blessings than we could ever imagine! Not by giving us more, but by helping us to see what we have with different eyes. Sisters, whatever the Lord has seen fit to bless us with is enough. It will *always* be enough if we fully rely on Christ to lift us above the temporal concerns of life and look heavenward into the eternities. Ask the Lord to heal you of the desire to seek after vain imaginations, and he will.

3. Service. "But wilt thou know, O vain [woman], that faith without works is dead?" (James 2:20). Haven't you always heard that the best cure when you're feeling down about yourself and your lot in life is to serve someone? If you have ever put this theory to the test, you know it works. When we are feeling "less than" we need to find someone to serve. Serving others is the way we show the Lord we love Him, that we are grateful for Him, and that we are true followers of Christ. I have never had an experience serving someone when I didn't come away feeling full! Full of love, full of gratitude, full of life! Happy about my circumstances. And content with my physical body.

WALK AWAY FROM VANITY

Although the world constantly tempts us to walk towards vanity . . . we must choose to walk away. If we vigilantly put into practice prayers of gratitude, the Atonement of Christ, and put our hands to work in the service of God, we will strengthen our ability to resist the adversary's temptations of vanity. To be honest, resisting will be something we will have to do not just once but over and over again. But with persistence and resistance we can and will overcome!

How blessed we are to have eternal truths to guide and direct us in our beauty pursuits. Living prophets and apostles have taught and will continue to teach us the doctrine of the body. Drawing upon the powers of God, and by following the counsel of our leaders, let us fill our lives with the goodness and mercy of Jesus Christ. As we strive to love the way we look, allow Christ to fill the well within you full of living water (D&C 63:23). For His well will never go dry.

NOTES

1. Susan W. Tanner, "The Sanctity of the Body," *Liahona*, Nov. 2005, 13.

2. Holland, "To Young Women."

3. Ibid. Emphasis added.

4. Ibid. Emphasis added.

5. Henry Wadsworth Longfellow, "A Psalm of Life," http://www.bartleby.com/102/55.html.

6. James Allen, *As a Man Thinketh* (Salt Lake City: Deseret Book, 2002), 9.

7. Boyd K. Packer, "Children of God," In *Rise to the Divinity Within You* (Salt Lake City: Deseret Book, 2007), 2.

8. Holland and Holland, "What Time is This?"

13

The Beauty of Working Together as Sisters in Christ

INTELLIGENCE CLEAVETH UNTO INTELLIGENCE; WISDOM RECEIVETH WISDOM;
TRUTH EMBRACETH TRUTH; VIRTUE LOVETH VIRTUE.
—Doctrine and Covenants 88:40

I was in my early twenties when I heard President Howard W. Hunter state the following in a 1994 General Relief Society meeting: "Our Lord and Savior looked to the women of his time for a comforting hand . . . a believing heart [and] loyalty." So do His servants today. President Hunter continued: "There is a great need to rally the women of the Church today to stand with and for the Brethren in stemming the tide of evil that surrounds us and in moving forward the work of our Savior."[1] I have heard this statement repeated in many talks and lessons and every time it still gives me delightful chills! How I would love to have been a woman who walked and talked with Christ. I can see Mary and Martha in mind, sitting upon their dirt-covered floor eyes gazing at Christ as He teaches them. I can see Mary Magdalene approaching Christ with wonderment in her eyes saying, "Is it you, dear Lord? Is it really you?" I can see his mother Mary gently advising him, encouraging him, and tenderly comforting him as only a mother could do. In 1994, I wanted to know how I could be like the women who loved and supported Jesus. I knew they walked and talked with Christ, and if I wanted to someday do the same, I needed to be like them. We become like them by supporting his servants, by standing together in the cause of Christ.

President Hunter's call for us to *"stand with and for the Brethren in stemming the tide of evil"* is *still* relevant today—perhaps even more so as the world turns more wicked. It is important that women seeking to walk in paths of virtue heed this call from a prophet of God. It is important that virtue-seeking women choose to stand fast together for the cause of virtue. It is imperative that women of faith stand firm in their faith to further the work of the Savior. So I ask you: are you ready to do your part?

In the first chapter of the Epistle of Paul to the Philippians, we read, "Stand fast in one spirit, with one mind striving together for the faith of the gospel" (Philippians 1:27). Sisters, let us be "one spirit" and "one mind." If we are going to rise up to this great challenge to bring about virtue in are own lives and the lives of our loved ones, we have to come together. We can't shimmy back and forth, thinking our choices will have no bearing on our children's choices and generations to come. If we are going to change "the dismal situation in which we are sliding"; if we are going to become a powerful force for good; if we are going to lead future sons and daughters by showing them how to live lives of virtue, then we must *live* lives of virtue; and we must do it together. We must hold hands and be one!

I look at daughters of God joining together in the cause of virtue in this way. If one virtuous woman lives virtuously and she is holding on to two other virtuous women, who are holding on to two other virtuous women, and so on, and so on, soon we will become a great and undeniable force fighting in and on behalf of virtue, who is our Lord and Savior Jesus Christ. Just think about it. "Intelligence cleaveth unto intelligence; wisdom receiveth wisdom; truth embraceth truth; virtue loveth virtue" (D&C 88:40). We will be drawn to each other and others will be drawn to us because of our light. To do this, we must require the best of ourselves and then require the best in others. Let our voices be heard in the cause of virtue. Let our actions be seen in the cause of shunning evil of all kinds. I pray that, as women of virtue, we will stand apart and be leaders among our family members, friends, neighbors, and associates. Let us cleave to one another and strengthen one another that we may "all sit down in heaven together."[2]

As a virtuous body of women, Christ will give us strength to do whatever we must do to bring about virtuous change. One of the Savior's best characteristics was His ability to accept "others as they were without the intention to leave them as they were."[3] Isn't this just a beautiful thought! This is how we must conduct ourselves. We must leave others better than we found them. And that requires each of us to be at our very best.

For the sake of our daughters, our sons, our grandchildren, and great-grandchildren, and children not yet born, we, the daughters of the noble birthright—no matter how young, no matter how old, no matter our socioeconomic status, no matter the burdens placed upon us—we must realize our divine potential. We must realize we have been given a responsibility to lift ourselves and others out of the mists of darkness, to rise above them, and move beyond them. By the virtue of who we are, as spirit daughters of the Almighty God, and as sisters in Christ, we can and will accomplish amazing things if we are true to our virtue.

Don't Underestimate the Power of Virtuous Women

Let us not underestimate our influence as virtuous women. Remember that one glowing candle gives plenty of light to edge away the darkness in a blackened room; and one tiny seed grows into a beautiful flower taking up space where a weed may have grown. Be that little light willing to glow. Be that tiny, little seed willing to grow. M. Russell Ballard said: "Every sister who stands for truth and righteousness diminishes the influence of evil . . . . Every sister who lives as a woman of God becomes a beacon for others to follow and plants seeds of righteous influence that will be harvested for decades to come."[4]

As Young Women and Relief Society sisters, we are five plus million women bound by a vision of virtue leading to eternal possibilities. Working together, with a unified vision of virtue, we can help our priesthood brethren stem the tide of evil and help move forward the work of our beloved Savior. Let us "gather together whatsoever force [we] can upon [our] march hither, and we will go speedily against those dissenters, in the strength of our God according to the faith which is in us" (Alma 61:17). Let us unite! Jesus Christ said, "If ye are not one ye are not mine" (D&C 38:27). "And if a house be divided against itself, that house cannot stand" (Mark 3:25). But, if we are united, we can stand against the world!

> Father, if You need a woman to rear children in righteousness, here am I, send me. If You need a woman who will shun vulgarity and dress modestly and speak with dignity and show the world how joyous it is to keep the commandments, here am I, send me. If You need a woman

who can resist the alluring temptations of the world by keeping her eyes fixed on eternity, here am I, send me. If You need a woman of faithful steadiness, here am I, send me. Between now and the day the Lord comes again, He needs women in every family, in every ward, in every community, in every nation who will step forward in righteousness and say by their words and their actions, "Here am I, send me."[5]

Will *you* be one of the women who responds, "Yes! Father, here I am, send me." When asked if we all will stand together as virtuous women of God, helping to bring up righteous generations unto the Lord, how can we not say emphatically, "Yes! Here we are, Lord! Send us!"

RALLYING THE STRENGTH OF OUR SISTERS

We can't prevent evil, but we can rally against it by joining together as sisters in Christ. There is divine power in our sisterhood. The scriptures tell us, when we are converted to go and strengthen our brothers and sisters (Luke 22:32). And so, let's get on with it! Let's strengthen each other and then strengthen our family, our neighbor, our sister, our friend, our coworker, our world. Remember, we have the strength and honor of Jesus Christ on our side. We have the truthfulness and fulness of the gospel. What else could give us the confidence we need to excel as virtuous women *in* the world but not *of* the world? What more could give us the courage than a call from our Savior, asking us to use our virtuous influence to bring about his righteous purposes?

Our power to influence virtue among our fellow brothers and sisters is only as strong as our convictions and our integrity to act upon them. President Hinckley believed that we should stand together and stand tall: "Stand tall and be strong in defense of those great virtues which have been the backbone of our social progress. When you are united, your power is limitless. You can accomplish anything you wish to accomplish. And oh, how very, very great is the need for you in a world of crumbling values where the adversary seems so very much to be in control."[6]

IN CLOSING

Has someone ever told you, "There is just something different about you. I can't quite put my finger on it. But something is different." This *something* is what the world needs more of. This something is your virtue, your goodness. And it shines in your countenance and radiates through your soul.

We have enough women of the world. We need more women of virtue. Former Young Women General President Margaret D. Nadauld said: "We have enough women of fame and fortune; we need more women of faith. We have enough greed; we need more goodness. We have enough vanity; we need more virtue. We have enough popularity; we need more purity."[7] We need more women of virtue! By virtue we will become all that we are and must be!

How do you become a woman of virtue? It has been said of the brilliant and masterful sculptor Michelangelo that he chiseled away day and night, month after month, until eventually, Moses emerged from the stone. When a man asked Michelangelo how he had created such a masterpiece, he humbly replied, "I just chiseled away until everything that wasn't Moses wasn't there."[8] Like a sculptor, a virtuous woman will carve out a more virtuous character by chiseling away anything and everything that isn't virtuous.

Diminishing virtues are the ways of the world, but not the ways of women who believe in the beauty of virtue. They are women who love the Lord. They know the worth of a virtuous woman is priceless; that they are more precious than rubies (Proverbs 31:10). They have charitable hearts and are anxiously engaged in good works. They rally together to bear one another's burdens. They seek to be distinct and different from the women of the world. They find joy in the virtuous things of God. Our prophets have taught us that "no greater recognition can come to [us] in this world than to be known as a woman of God."[9] Let us seek to have this kind of recognition.

Let us not deviate from those things that have eternal value. Let us hold sacred all that is virtuous and place the highest allegiance to living a life of purity and virtue, and teach others by our example and good works to do likewise. May we recognize that it is our responsibility to stand against the adversary in an effort to preserve all that is virtuous, lovely, and praiseworthy. Our greatest defense against the adversary lies in the integrity of our virtue. Let us maintain an unwavering commitment to lead the next generation in righteousness by the virtue of who we are divinely as daughters of the Almighty God!

Rise, up! Oh, women of Zion! One by one, sister by sister, woman by woman, holding hands and working together, let us believe in who we are! Let us *believe in the beauty of virtue.*

Notes

1. Howard W. Hunter, "Stand Firm in the Faith," *Ensign,* Nov. 1994, 96.

2. Lucy Mack Smith, as quoted in Kathleen H. Hughes, "That We May All Sit Down Together," *Liahona,* Nov. 2005, 110.

3. Marion D. Hanks, "Be and Not Seem," *BYU Speeches,* 23 January, 1979.

4. Ballard, "Women of Righteousness."

5. Ibid.

6. Gordon B. Hinckley, "Your Greatest Challenge, Mother," *Ensign,* Nov. 2000, 97.

7. Margaret D. Nadauld, "The Joy of Womanhood," *Ensign*, Nov. 2000, 14.

8. Max L. Pinegar, "Serious About the Things to Be Done," *BYU Speeches*, 11 April 1978.

9. Kimball, "The Role of Righteous Women."

About the Author

Jodi Robinson resides in Riverton, Utah, with her husband and four children. She has been married for over seventeen years. She is a free-lance writer and public speaker. Jodi received the Salt Lake County Volunteer of the Year Award for her work with the women at a center that helps women recovering from addiction. She refers to these women as her "heroes" and sees firsthand how women transform their lives by living more virtuously. She has served as a Relief Society president, Young Women president, and Young Women's advisor as well as other various callings.